Beginner's Guide to
CRUISING

Aaron Mase

ISBN: 1-4392-0801-8
ISBN-13: 9781439208014

Visit www.booksurge.com to order additional copies.

I want to dedicate this book to my cruising companion; my wife Paula, who encouraged me to put into print all the disorganized thoughts and experiences I have had and have offered fellow cruisers.

Also, thanks to the kids (Jafa, Cujo, Bear, and Tasha) for putting up with our absences.

TABLE OF CONTENTS

CHAPTER 1

DECIDING ON A CRUISE VACATION

Choosing a vacation can be an overwhelming task as one endeavors to find the perfect vacation choice that "has it all": affordability, great weather, favorite activities, scenery, food, and ease of getting to the chosen vacation destination. A lot of vacationers choose the "all-inclusive" resort vacations to help minimize the effort in planning. After all, it's not a lot of fun if hard work is needed to plan and experience the event that most of us are lucky enough to experience once a year. An all-inclusive resort takes care of all the planning and logistics for you, combining room, board, air and sometimes an excursion in one easy to calculate price.

A cruise vacation IS your all-inclusive resort (with a few exceptions discussed later) with one major, unique exception: it glides along the sea with leisurely speed from one exotic destination to the next. If you are interested in paying one price for the majority of all your vacation needs, if you are interested in visiting more than one island or country on your vacation but are less than excited about making air arrangements for each place, if you are interested in an unlimited choice of dining pleasures, then a cruise may be something for you to consider for your next vacation.

Cruise lines of today are almost unrecognizable compared to 30 years ago when a cruise vacation was featured Saturday evenings on the television set, which allowed us one hour of escape and wonder. We watched and wondered how great a cruise vacation must be and how nice it would be to enjoy such an experience. Unfortunately, for most of us, we either could not afford a cruise back then, or we felt we were too young for a cruise, or we thought we would be too bored and were not excited with the concept of being "stuck" within the confines of a ship at sea. Cruise lines, cruise ships, cruise destinations, and cruise activities have a totally different look today and offer something for everyone. The problem is taking that first cruise. Less than 20% of the population has taken a cruise and most of that percentage is repeat passengers. Most people are still apprehensive about taking a cruise. It seems that the news never has anything positive to report; but then it would not be news. Check out a few magazines dedicated to cruising and watch a few travel shows that are about cruising and you can get a feel for that which is not reported in the media.

Cruises are available to fit every budget. There are cruises that sail 2 day, 3 day, 4 day, 5 day, 6 day, 7 day and 8 day cruises. You can also choose a 10 day, 14 day, 21 day cruise or longer. Part of your cruise pricing will be based on length of cruise, as any other vacation. The cruise lines offer multiple options to fit the busy everyday lifestyle we all have. From a quick getaway weekend to a long leisurely world cruise of three plus months, the cruise lines have it covered. Destinations are also endless as you can cruise the Caribbean, Mediterranean, Alaska, Hawaiian Islands, the South Pacific and Asia. That list is only the beginning of where you can cruise. Incidentally, your cruise destination will also be a determining factor in your cruise price. As with any vacation you take, in which driving is not a consideration, you will have to consider airfare in your plans. Cruise lines will take care of this for you also, thereby lessening your stress and time in finding and booking airfare for your cruise. The cruise line's price of airfare is often a little more (sometimes a lot more) than what you can book on your own. You do not have to purchase the cruise line's airfare, but in a lot of cases it makes the most sense to let them do all the work. Here is why: if you allow the cruise line to purchase your air, the cruise line is responsible for any air cancellations and any airline changes to the air itinerary as far as getting you to the ship. The cruise line books blocks of seats several months in advance of your cruise at a discount rate from the airline. Depending on when you decide to book your air reservations (if you do this on your own), you may find it difficult to find any seats available. If you purchase your own air arrangement and there happens to be a cancellation or a change in your air itinerary, you will have the unfortunate pleasure of finding a suitable alternative that will ensure your arrival at the port in time to board your cruise.

Once you have decided that a cruise is for you and you make the commitment to venture into the cruise experience, you will want to decide the length of your cruise, the destination of your cruise, and the cruise line and ship for your cruise vacation. Every cruise line has its own demographic and each ship has its own personality. These decisions and many other considerations for your first cruise will be discussed in the following chapters in the hope that some of the myths and some of the apprehension of taking a cruise can be explained to put you at ease with cruising.

CHAPTER 2

CHOOSING THE RIGHT ITINERARY FOR YOU

Where do you want to go? That is the big question. In deciding any vacation, price is always a factor and as with land vacations, cruise vacations are priced according to demand and popularity. If you want to vacation in the world's most popular destinations at the most popular time of the year, price will be higher with any vacation you are planning and cruises are no exception. Warm destinations in the winter and cooler climates in the summer are the optimum peak seasons and itineraries. No matter when you want to cruise, with advance planning and careful consideration you will be able to find a cruise vacation that meets your definition of value.

Cruise lines have opened the world to cruisers. Each year, the cruise lines offer more itineraries and options overseas in an attempt to satisfy the growing demand for summer cruising outside of the Caribbean area. Europe is a fast growing cruise market with some cruise lines positioning ships year round in the Mediterranean. Alaska is still popular in the May - September cruising season. Bermuda is still on some cruise line's summer options. The government of Bermuda controls the number of cruises calling on the island. Certain cruise lines make Bermuda cruises a part of their weekly itineraries and some make a few choice stops along the way. The Caribbean is still popular in the summer, with fewer ships as a lot are positioned in Europe, Alaska, and the overseas markets in Australia and Asia to name a couple. Naturally, hurricanes are a consideration in the summer months as the official hurricane season runs from June through November. For a getaway weekend most of the 3 day and 4 day cruises head for the warm waters of the Bahamas for these short jaunts. This is a great choice to "get your feet wet" and experience a cruise to see if this is something you may enjoy as a week long vacation. Most of these cruises are scheduled as long weekend cruises so you can minimize your time away from work, minimize your investment if you are still unsure if a cruise is your style, and a great way to maximize fun in a short period of time. It is also a great way to rest and relax and recharge your batteries if you feel like doing nothing in an inviting chair, with a cold drink in your hand and an ocean breeze circulating around you on the ship's open deck.

Caribbean itineraries - The most popular cruise choice and the one that is conjured up when thinking of cruising. There are as many different itineraries in the Caribbean as there are ships sailing them. The most popular are called Eastern Caribbean, Western Caribbean, and Southern Caribbean. Most Eastern Caribbean cruises include stops at San Juan, St Thomas and St Maarten. These cruises are usually 7 days long and include a stop at two or more islands intermingled with a couple of days at sea for your relaxing pleasure. Some cruise lines own their own private island and one of your stops will be on one of these unpopulated islands; unpopulated until the ship arrives and then it will be an exclusive getaway for you to enjoy. The islands featured on these itineraries are some of the most popular islands and the islands themselves are ready for cruise passengers with expanding infrastructures to accommodate the surge of passengers when the ships call. On the Western Caribbean itinerary, the most popular islands visited are Cozumel, Grand Cayman, and Jamaica. All are favorites and have a lot to offer from shopping, snorkeling, 4-wheel exploring, sight-seeing to zip lining across the jungle canopy. As far as private islands, the Eastern Caribbean itineraries will offer a better chance of a visit as most ships depart from the East coast of Florida and have more time available in the itinerary to allow a stop at the private island. There are a few sailings to the Western Caribbean that do feature a stop at a private island. If the Western Caribbean and a private island are of interest, you do have limited choices, but it is available. Just check in the cruise line's brochures or with your cruise/travel agent. Itineraries are subject to change and this is something that is not set in stone. For the Eastern and Western Caribbean itineraries, most of the cruise ships depart from Florida. A few depart from Louisiana and Texas. Cruises departing from Texas, Louisiana, Alabama, and Western Florida offer mostly Western Caribbean itineraries. As far as Southern Caribbean itineraries, most originate from San Juan, which allows a cruise ship to reach islands further south in the Caribbean in a 7 or 10 day itinerary allowing passengers to explore islands that are too far to be reached by cruise ships leaving from Florida on 7 day voyages. Aruba, Grenada, Barbados, St. Lucia, Dominica and Antigua are some of the more popular islands cruise ships visit on Southern Caribbean itineraries. While you can cruise the Caribbean year round, you are limited to the number of varying itineraries in the summer months as ships are moved from the Caribbean to other destinations throughout the world. During the summer months your options of departure cities in the U.S. do increase. New York offers year round cruising to the Caribbean, but more sailings are offered from Philadelphia, Baltimore, Norfolk, Charleston, and New Jersey during the summer months as the weather is much more compatible in these cities. It is a very interesting voyage when taking a cruise from New York in the middle of January. You may leave the pier bundled up with a cup of hot cocoa with snow on the decks and as your ship proceeds south, you start shedding the layers as the snow melts off of the ship. The increased number of cruise offerings, among the cities along the East Coast, allows cruisers more options in choosing their cruise departure city. The cruise lines call this *home port* cruising and it was a project that was explored after the tragedy of 9-11. Allowing more passengers a driving alternative to flying, the cruise lines were able to reach more markets and made cruising more convenient. Any time airlines experience capacity issues or any time the public would rather avoid flying, these home port cruises offer a more economical means of affording a cruise vacation by avoiding the cost of airfare while still enjoying the pleasure of cruising.

European itineraries - There are a number of ships that spend the summer cruising the waters of Europe. The option of ship choices and cruise destinations continues to grow each year. You can cruise in the north and in the south with many varied itineraries that allow a wide selection of choices for differing tastes. You can choose cruises that concentrate on the Greek Isles. You can choose a cruise that offers Italy and Spain. You can cruise the Baltic. You can select a cruise that includes Great Britain and Ireland. There are cruises that sail from England to the Canary Islands, Portugal, and Spain. You can sail from Barcelona to Greece to Egypt and Cyprus. The options for cruising Europe have just scratched the surface. The cruise lines all have their own idea as to what each area of Europe they are cruising should be called in their itinerary. What one cruise line calls a northern European cruise can mean something else to another cruise line, each having different ports of call, but in the same region. The cruise line's brochures will provide you with the specific itineraries and ports of call. New cruise ships being built that have a timely christening coinciding with the beginning of summer are being positioned in Europe for the summer to offer cruisers a new ship to explore. Along with the new ship comes new itineraries and cruise lines are expanding their European voyages each year with new ports of call and new variations to their itineraries to give passengers the most of Europe in one cruise. If cruising of today looks different than it did 30 years ago, Europe definitely is looking different than it did 10 years ago. As cruise lines look at new destinations for their new ships, European cruises are in high demand from Americans and Europeans. Cruise lines are offering their newer and larger ships to this area for the summer months to compete with one another and to offer passengers more variety. As the cruise lines offer more ships, they are creating new itineraries to accompany those ships and are visiting places that have not been on the cruising schedule in the past and the cruise passengers are benefiting from this expansion. Cruise lengths in Europe vary from the traditional 7 days to 14 days and longer.

Alaska itineraries – Most of the major cruise lines position at least one of their ships to take advantage of the Alaska cruise season. Europe is rivaling Alaska as a summer cruise destination, but the cruise lines are sending more ships and larger ships each season to Alaska. You can sail Alaska as early as May and as late as September. Pricing will be higher in the middle of the season as the weather is nicer. I cannot tell you the best month to go as I do not even know. One week it will be shorts and t-shirt and the next week it will be jacket weather. I have been told June is a great month. I have been told that July is the time to go. I have also been told that August is warm. I decided to travel in early August. It was not warm. It was cold and windy and wet. I still had a great time, but I am not confidant that anyone knows when it is the right time to go. It seems that the people you talk to always had nice weather. I wonder if anyone who says that was on my August cruise and remembers the weather. The most important aspect is that Alaska, no matter how wet, windy, or cold is beautiful. Just remember it is still Alaska and the cold, wind, and rain are weather norms. You can visit Alaska and wear shorts and t-shirts the whole cruise, but no matter what your itinerary, the chances of visiting a glacier are great and the weather associated with that area of Alaska will fit the excursion. Most cruise ships sail out of Vancouver or Seattle and offer 7-14 day cruises. The most popular ports of call are Ketchikan, Juneau, Skagway, and a scenic cruise near a glacier. The weather and the number of ice chunks floating in the bay will determine how close your cruise ship can get to the glacier. The chance of getting closer to the moving glacier is better with the smaller ships. The number of cruise ships, the varying size of cruise ships, and the number of cruise lines sailing Alaska each year vary, but your choices are abundant and currently there are more than enough options to choose from in deciding your itinerary and ship size.

Bermuda - Bermuda was mentioned in the Caribbean itineraries, but select cruise lines offer cruises to Bermuda. These cruises are just that - cruises to Bermuda. A 7 day cruise consists of sea days and the rest of the week is spent in Bermuda. Unlike other cruises, which offer more than one island, these offer one island: Bermuda. The ship is still at your service and still your home while you explore all the island has to offer - day and night.

Trans-Panama Canal - These cruises sail from East Coast to the West Coast and the opposite through the Panama Canal allowing passengers the experience of the day long transit of the locks and dams of the canal. These cruises are for the most part longer than 7 days as the ships visit several ports of call along one of the coasts. Some of these cruises are called repositioning cruises as the cruise ship may be moving from the Caribbean to Alaska for the summer months. The reverse cruise in the fall will have the ship returning to the Caribbean. You can usually find some great pricing on these repositioning cruises so check with your agent if you think this is an option for you to explore.

South Pacific and Australia - These cruises are niche cruises and are not always available year round. The travel time to the ship's destination results in a longer cruise voyage so you need to plan ahead to have plenty of time to enjoy these cruises to exotic ports of call. Not all cruise lines include these places in their itineraries. If you are serious about traveling here, find some brochures to review as to which cruise lines are offering these cruises and what cruises are available as the itineraries and the ships available are always changing. Most of these areas have a peak season so cruise lines will position one or two ships in these areas to accommodate the demand for these cruises. The itineraries are extensive and cover many different ports of call. This creates itineraries longer than the typical 7 days. These types of cruises are usually called "exotic" and visit those places that we consider our dream vacation destinations. You will spend extra time just traveling to your ship than you would normally spend flying to a cruise in the Caribbean so prices will be higher, but don't let that discourage you. When you figure how much this cruise would cost per day versus the Caribbean, you will be able to find some very reasonably priced sailings.

Mexican Riviera - This cruise was the cruise of choice on the famous TV show and includes stops at Acapulco, Mazatlan, Cabo San Lucas, and Puerto Vallarta to name the popular. Most of these sailings originate in Los Angeles. Some cruises sail from San Diego, Long Beach, or San Francisco. Not all cruise lines offer these itineraries, but you can experience 4 to 12 day cruises in this area. Your options are a little more limited as there are only a few ships that sail this itinerary every week. Cruise lines do rotate ships every couple of years so that cruisers, especially living on the West Coast, can have variety and experience the latest trends and amenities found onboard cruise ships.

South America - Cruise lines are starting to explore this area for new cruise itineraries allowing their passengers more options in cruising different parts of the globe. Not all cruise lines are sailing these itineraries and most cruises are at least 10 days in length with most being longer. As this is a new area for the cruise lines to explore, there will be many changes to ships and itineraries as the demand changes and port choices become popular. Cruise lines experiment with new destinations and if they become a success, the cruises become more plentiful as other cruise lines start offering similar sailings to compete in the area and the original cruise lines offer more ships and choices.

East Coast Fall Cruising - During the fall foliage season, several cruise lines position ships in this area so passengers can enjoy the beauty of autumn and the changing leaves. Cruise ships of all sizes offer these cruises and your options keep getting better each year. Just remember, every season is a little different and sometimes the leaves stay green a little longer than perhaps other years, so make sure you plan on enjoying the ship and ports of call as much as the changing of the leaves. Nature is fickle in this area just as it is in the Caribbean during the summer season, so plan accordingly. These cruises sail from the East Coast, so driving to the ship may be an affordable option if you choose this cruise.

Other cruises- You can still enjoy a Trans Atlantic cruise on a cruise line that sails between Southampton, England and New York City. Other cruise lines may sail this route as a repositioning cruise, but those are seasonal and only once or twice a year. You may perhaps enjoy a world cruise if you have the time and budget. World cruises are 90+ days in length, but cruise lines do offer you the option of sailing segments of the cruise in varying lengths of days. Cruise lines are exploring the Asia market as a new, fast growing cruise area and will be adding more ships as the demand warrants. It appears the Asia market is receptive to cruising so the future appears to have room for growth for the cruise lines.

As you can see, the world is available on a cruise vacation and as cruising continues to grow and as cruise lines explore new areas to cruise, some of the less explored cruising regions will be accessible by more cruise lines and cruise ships. Just as Europe has exploded as a cruise region, other areas that are gaining popularity (Asia and South America) will be offering more options for cruisers. The vast number of cruise options is not meant to be intimidating; they are available for your vacation experience to suit your desire for exploration. Along the way of your exploration, you can experience the cruising environment and let the cruise also be part of your vacation experience.

In deciding on any itinerary, not only do you want to choose something you would enjoy, you will want to choose something to fit your budget. You will want to choose the length of cruise you think would be suitable for your vacation experience. The itinerary you choose should be one that will fit your schedule and budget. You should know the climate for the itinerary you are choosing so you may experience the time of year that offers the greatest chance of good weather.

You will want to consider the number of sea days and the number of days in port. Depending on your preference, you may want to be in a different port each day or you may prefer more sea days on your vacation. Depending on where you live, you may choose to drive to the port where your ship will be leaving. The cruise lines offer many options in departure cities, length of cruise, diversity of itineraries, and size of ships. All these options are to make your choice easier as cruise lines have more to offer than ever before.

A small note I think is worth mentioning as you choose an itinerary is what is called tendering. Tendering is the procedure by which the passengers leave the ship on a "tender" (a life boat size vessel) and are transported to shore. This is done for a couple of reasons: one is that the island/city you are visiting has no dock or pier to accommodate your ship, no matter how small your ship. In this day and age, it sounds odd with the popularity of cruising, that there are no docking facilities. There may not be a pier as this particular island/city does not receive a lot of ships as the island's infrastructure cannot handle a large number of people, or the island may be surrounded by a protected coral reef and building pier facilities would damage the fragile eco-system. The second reason could be that there are not enough piers to handle all the incoming ships, so certain vessels will have to use tenders to transport the passengers to shore. As cruise lines look for new places to visit (especially in the Caribbean), they are investing more money into an island's economy and building piers to accommodate ships so passengers can enjoy the convenience of walking off the ship onto shore, instead of the sometimes long process of tendering. This may be something you want to consider and keep in mind when selecting a ship for your cruise vacation (discussed in the next chapter). There are some islands on which you will have to tender as they have no pier to accommodate any ship, and there are some islands that cannot handle the larger ships, so the larger ships will have to tender passengers as the pier is not deep enough to accommodate the larger vessels. Tendering should not determine whether you cruise or vacation on land, but it is something to keep in mind when planning a vacation. It could determine your ship choice or itinerary choice.

CHAPTER 3

CHOOSING THE RIGHT SHIP FOR YOU

Cruise ships/ships come in all sizes. You can take a cruise on a small ship carrying less than 100 passengers or you can take a cruise on a "mega-liner" carrying more than 5,000 passengers or you can take a cruise on any other varying size of ship in between. Most of the major cruise lines have many ships, all varying in size, allowing the consumer a wide range of choices. What is considered as a small ship today (600 passengers) would be the norm 30 years ago. The mega-liners of today were unthinkable 30 years ago. As each new generation of ship was constructed, new technologies were created and advancements made so the next generation of ship could be made a little bit bigger reaching the point we are today. Currently, (as of this writing) there are ships being built that have few places to go as island and port infrastructure cannot accommodate these behemoths. By the time these new ships set sail (2009), new piers will have been built, current facilities upgraded, and island infrastructures altered to accommodate not only these large ships, but the large number of passengers they will carry. As new ships have been constructed over the years, new designs have been implemented to accommodate growing consumer tastes (some of which will be discussed in later chapters), such as more cabins with balconies. Again, new technologies, and new lessons learned have allowed ship yards and cruise lines to build a floating entertainment arena. I am not sure you can call them "floating hotels" anymore, as cruise ships are more than a means of transportation from one place to the next. They are a vacation adventure. Just as Las Vegas is no longer just a place to gamble, it is advertised as a vacation for the whole family, so too are cruises. And family vacation has taken on a new meaning in the cruise industry as so many cruise lines offer great children's/teen's programs so there is something for everyone.

Cruising style varies from cruise line to cruise line and differs among ships of the same company. There are cruise lines that cater to a younger crowd and are more adventurous and geared more to the outgoing type. There are cruise lines that are more upscale and the passengers taking those cruises tend to be older. You can choose a cruise line that is in between the two styles and there are many that vary in degree from casual to more formal and outgoing to more conservative. You can sail on a very luxurious line in which not only will the crowd tend to be older, but the ship will be more than casual and dressing up will be a common way of life. You can choose a cruise of this style and have your champagne and caviar delivered to you in the wading surf. If this is your kind of vacation, there are several great lines that offer that personal touch and will cater to your personal needs. The ships tend to be small, the passengers are few with the crew size being comparable to the number of passengers so you experience that personal catered to service that sets the other cruise lines apart. If that is not your personality, you can choose a more casual cruise where mixed drinks will be brought to you (for a fee) while sunning on a beach somewhere, but no caviar in the surf. You will still experience great service, but the passengers outnumber the crew so you will not be on a first name basis with every crew member, but that does not mean it will be a bad vacation. The longer length cruises tend to attract an older crowd (especially the world cruises) as those passengers have more time available to them to use for vacations. The more exotic cruises will attract a more experienced, older crowd. This is not to say that we cruisers are not welcome on these voyages, but most of us do not have the time or money to experience the far-away lands that we dream about, so we enjoy the same pleasures taking a shorter length cruise closer to home and we are able to enjoy the same experience that makes us comfortable and allows us to relax. The shorter cruises (3–5 day) tend to attract a younger crowd as these cruises are great for a weekend getaway. They are also a great way to get your feel for a cruise to see if investing in a longer cruise vacation is in your future. The shorter cruises attract the larger size vessels so you will find a lot more passengers enjoying a cruise vacation. If you are not looking for large crowds, you may want to search for a smaller cruise ship. Sometimes, these turn out to be a pleasant surprise as the smaller ships can sail to places that the big ships cannot. The smaller ships tend to have fewer amenities and activities, but they make up for this in ambiance and itinerary. If you are fine with large groups of people or even just a lot of fellow vacationers, then your selection of cruise ships has just exponentially increased and you will be able to have the itinerary you want and the ship, too. The itinerary you choose may determine the size of ship for your cruise. If you decide to enjoy a Caribbean vacation on a ship, you will have the greatest choice of size and the greatest choice of cruising style.

The Caribbean is popular even during the summer months and various ships will be sailing different itineraries. The 7 day cruise is the most popular as this length of cruise fits into most everyone's vacation plans so this length of cruise comprises most cruise lines itineraries. During the winter months you will have your choice of cruise line and cruise ship as this is peak season so the cruise lines position the most ships in the Caribbean. You will be able to choose any style of cruising you prefer in any length on any size of ship in the Caribbean. This may be the best place to try your first cruise. While no one can guarantee perfect weather, the Caribbean does offer the sun and warmth we crave during the winter months and the Caribbean has the beaches and warm water we desire. You can experience white sand, black sand, pink sand, coarse sand, or baby powder sand. Blue skies, palm trees, warm rays of the sun, and beautiful sunsets all can be had at any resort vacation; on a cruise you have the wonderful alternative of experiencing all of this on more than one island while your "resort" transports you to each locale.

European cruises have grown in popularity and today you have more than a couple of options when it comes to ship size and style. Alaska cruises are still popular and cruise lines are sending many ships of varying sizes and varying styles to satisfy all passengers. When you start reaching beyond these destinations, your selection of ships, in size and style, diminish. Some of the other regions of the globe determine the size of ship sailing as the islands may not have the infrastructure to accommodate large vessels. Some of these areas, while popular, are not in high demand as the Caribbean, Europe, or Alaska so it is easier for the cruise line to fill a smaller vessel. Some of these cruises are only offered a few times a year based on demand and peak seasons. As discussed in the previous chapter, some of these less visited areas do not have the port structure so your ship will have to tender the passengers to shore. In many cases, the smaller ships fit very nicely in these itineraries.

As you are considering the size of ship, you will need to determine what type of vacation you want to experience. Will this be a family vacation? If so, you will want to select those cruise lines and ships that have great children's programs and allow for the most options for a family vacation. Your itinerary will also be part of this process, as your island choices and choices ashore will mean different things if you are looking for a family vacation as opposed to a vacation for two. There are some cruise lines that are known for catering to families, or family friendly, and others whose style of cruising is not conducive to a family style vacation. Of course, family does not just mean children, but when traveling with children, you will want to choose a cruise line that has an extensive children's program. A lot of cruise lines have made serious upgrades to their children's/ teen's programs and they are continuously being expanded.

Everyone has different tastes and styles and looks for different experiences to make their vacation memorable. There are those who like to stay up late and party through the night. There are those who are content to turn in early. Some want to be on the go all the time and others are more content to sit back and relax. All of this is available on a cruise and for the most part, all of this can be available on the same ship. Yes, some cruise lines have a reputation for being lively and you can be up all night enjoying the night life. There are those cruise lines that have a reputation for being more sedate and not so "outgoing" with the night life ending a little early. It depends on the type of passenger the cruise line attracts. Cruise ships are no different as some ships, based on entertainment venues, and ship's crew, have the party all night personality while other ships of the same cruise line are more laid back. In general, the style and ambiance of the ship reflects the style of the cruise line. That is what you need to choose: the cruise line that fits your needs and tastes, and the cruise ship itself will be chosen by selecting the size that fits your style. Remember, the larger the vessel the more passengers, but the more amenities and more choices of activities.

In choosing your ship and the size of ship, what you expect from the ship will determine the size. If you are more interested in the islands and a more laid back itinerary you could choose any size of ship you want because you can do nothing on any ship. If you are more interested in having a lot of activities because you are afraid that you will be BORED at sea, the larger ships offer more options. Cruise lines these days are pushing the imagination as to what you can find onboard a ship. Some have ice skating rinks where you can ice skate during the day and in the evening you can watch a choreographed show on ice. Some of the ships have rock climbing walls. Some ships have bowling alleys and boxing rings. There are ships where you can actually surf or learn to surf. Oh, the shuffleboard courts are present, but not in much use. Every so often you will see shuffleboard competitions. You can play basketball, volleyball, tennis, miniature golf, ping pong, or plunge down a water slide. Ships now have water parks that will help keep you entertained whether you are participating or just watching. There's virtual golf, a race car simulator, arcade games, and the ever popular sport of eating. Once that is done, you can burn off a few calories in the ship's ultra modern spa and gym. There are cooking demonstrations (more food), glass blowing, pottery making classes, wine tastings, martini tastings, champagne tastings, Vegas shows, art auctions, and towel folding demonstrations (not to learn how to fold a towel for your closet, but how to fold a towel into a towel animal, of course). There are guest lecturers on select cruises, comedians, magicians, jugglers, piano bars and guest talent shows.

As far as food, you can eat 24 hours a day. I am not sure that food would be a major reason to take a cruise, but most cruises feature culinary delights with many dining options. One of the more popular dining options which has become popular is "alternative dining". Cruise ships have specialty restaurants where you can dine and enjoy an untraditional dining experience. This is an option that does come with a fee to dine, currently around $20-30 per person. If you want to enjoy a special dining experience this is a very popular option that fills up fast and reservations are required. You can still dine at the buffet or in the main dining room or any other dining option, such as the deli, Chinese, Italian, the grill, or pizzeria. Most ships today require some form of dress code for dinner in the dining rooms. Most nights it is casual (no tee shirts or shorts). There are a couple of nights in which dressing up is required in the main dining room, but tuxes and ballroom gowns are not necessary for most dining experiences. In choosing the right ship for you, this may be a consideration. You can always enjoy the buffet in any dress style, but dining rooms on most ships still have a dress code and dining time. There are, however, a few ships from one cruise line in which there are no dress codes and there are no dining times. You can eat any time you would like (based on availability) in any one of the multiple themed dining rooms in casual resort wear. Again, this is something to consider if dressing up is just not your style in any circumstance. This choice may limit your itinerary and ship size, but it is your vacation and you want to be comfortable. Several cruise lines are experimenting with open dining, while still maintaining the traditional dining times for those who choose. Cruise lines are experimenting with more options for passengers in the dining area as far as dining times and options to accommodate passenger's requests.

Overwhelmed yet? Don't be. It is about choosing the various vacation options that are right for you. Once you have decided where you want to go and what ship is right for you, you need to think about accommodations. On a ship, they are not rooms, but cabins. There are different categories of cabins, but all you need to know are the basics to get started. There are inside cabins. These cabins have no windows. If you are not claustrophobic and/or do not need a window, this may be for you. These cabins are usually the most economical and sometimes the only feature they are missing to the next type of cabin is a window. The next category of cabin is an outside cabin. This cabin…has a window. The location of your cabin will determine if you have a square window (large or small) or a round porthole. The next category of cabin to know is an outside balcony cabin. This cabin has, naturally, a balcony. The type and location of the cabin you choose will determine the balcony size. The next cabin category is suite. You guessed it, this is a huge cabin with a balcony and, possibly, a hot tub. Easy enough, right? So, decide which style of cabin you want and then you can be more specific as to location or size. As you can guess, there are going to be multiple selections within each category. There are inside cabins with windows now, and on those ships these face an indoor promenade. There are different sizes of outside cabins, inside cabins, suites, and balcony cabins depending on their location on the ship. Once you decide on a category, you just refine your selection based on size and location. A point to remember, a cabin is not the same on all ships. This means that an outside cabin on one cruise line is not the same size as an outside cabin on another cruise line. Each cruise line is different. As cruise lines build newer ships, one of the trends is to make larger cabins for all passengers. Naturally, the more space a cabin requires the fewer cabins they can build and the fewer passengers can be accommodated. As ships grow larger, there is more room for newer amenities and still enough room to make larger cabins.

When considering these options, you first need to have an idea as to what kind of vacation you want to experience. Just as any land vacation, consideration to destination and the style of vacation is your first priority in choosing a cruise. As cruise lines have all vacation styles available this is your starting point. You would not want to take your three and five year olds with you to a romantic bungalow over the water in Bora Bora, the same goes for cruising. First consider where you want to go and then consider what type of vacation you want. If you have no idea where to start investigating what type of cruise would be right for you, contact your local travel or cruise agent and discuss what you are looking for. They will be able to help you with the itinerary choice and style and type of cruise ship that will make your vacation everything you expect. Once you have discussed this and narrowed your options, collect some brochures for those cruise lines and get a feel for the itineraries and the different ships. You will be able to look at the deck plans (like a house blueprint - only for ships). You can see some of the activities offered and be able to make a choice of cabin that you would desire. You will be able to see the various sizes of ships the cruise line has to offer for your itinerary and decide which one is right for you. It is also a great idea to go to the book store and purchase a couple of cruise magazines that are dedicated to cruising. This will allow you to get the feel for what is available. You can read comments sent in by readers and read articles about cruise ships and different ports of call. Most have a news update section with the latest trends and information about the cruise lines and what they are doing with ships, itineraries, and onboard activities. Your cruise selection process does not have to be made over night. This book is for beginner cruisers who may be having apprehensions about cruising, so don't be too hasty. Take your time. Read some magazines. Study some brochures that you think may interest you for your cruise vacation and keep asking questions of your agent. Check out some cruise websites that are chock full of cruise news, updates, itineraries, and cruise amenities. It is a great way to make you feel like a seasoned sailor and will not only help you answer some of your most intriguing thoughts, but will most of all, help you choose the right cruise and make the adventure more enjoyable. I always find that planning my next cruise is as enjoyable as taking the cruise.

CHAPTER 4

BOOKING YOUR CRUISE VACATION

After deciding your itinerary, the size of ship, and the style of cruise vacation, it is time to book your cruise. As mentioned in the previous chapter you can select a travel agent or a cruise agent. You can even use an online travel site and book your cruise online or you can book directly through the cruise line. I mentioned travel agent or cruise agent. There is a difference: a travel agent is an all encompassing vacation planner. They can book airfare, cruises, car rentals, hotels, etc. A cruise agent on the other hand specializes in cruises. A cruise agent usually has more knowledge about cruising and cruise lines and their ships as cruising is their business. That is not to say a well-traveled travel agent would not have as much experience. Having the advice and the knowledge of another human being in planning your first or second cruise is a great comfort and a great source of specific information you may request. Once you have settled on an agent and have picked a cruise do some last minute research before you book. Go online and read over the cruise line's website. Go onto travel websites or cruise websites and read the latest information. You can read a review of the ship you will be sailing; you can even read a review of the itinerary and places you will be visiting. Read a few cruise magazines and make sure you are comfortable in your choice. Read the cruise line's brochure. They have a few pages in the back of the brochure with the most commonly asked questions, and the answers to those questions are based on their ships. Remember, not all cruise lines are the same. They all offer a cruise vacation to wonderful destinations, but they all do it differently.

Now that you have made your decision, it is time to book. For those unfamiliar with cruising and all the options available, I would recommend booking with a travel agent or cruise agent. I, personally, enjoy the personal touch. The idea that I can call someone and have questions answered, problems solved, and receive great advice is why I have always booked my cruise with a travel agent or cruise agent. I have on two occasions booked directly through the cruise line with no problems, but I knew exactly what I wanted and did not need them for any specific information. I used the cruise line as at the time, they had some great offers I could not pass up, so I took advantage of their generous offers. When booking your cruise, there are a few fees that you need to know about. Cruises are advertised as "all-inclusive", but there are some things that are not included in your vacation price: soda, cocktails - let's just say most alcohol, unless you are booked on a luxury cruise ship - spa treatments, specialty dining restaurants, shore tours, and gift shop purchases. In booking your cruise you will be charged tax, of course. You will be charged port charges. For each one of your ports of call (island stops-city stops) you will be charged a fee. This varies from cruise line and is always changing. It's part of booking a cruise. You can book the cruise only portion of your cruise or book cruise and airfare. If you want to be as hands off as possible in booking this vacation, you may want to consider the cruise line's air. Airlines in turmoil are a major reason to let the cruise lines have all the headaches and hassles of getting you to the ship. If the airlines aren't the problem, but weather is an issue, guess who gets to rebook your flight to get you to the ship...? The cruise line! You do not have to deal with that hassle. Imagine if you are leaving Chicago in the middle of January and you have a delay because of snow...imagine this is on a Sunday when your agent is not working, or the website you booked from cannot help you at this late notice...relieve yourself of this stress and leave it in the cruise line's hands. I was booked on a cruise that happened to be one month after 9–11. I hesitated in going on the cruise because of the situation our country was in, but I went and I let the cruise line handle everything…what a relief. It was a great cruise. The air travel was horrible, as can be imagined, but it was not the fault of the cruise line. You can always avoid air all together by driving to the port, if it is within driving distance. Cruise lines are positioning ships all over the country to try and accommodate as many passengers as necessary by easing the burden of flying. Driving to the pier is one way to avoid the airline hassle and airfare. If you arrive by air, you will need to arrange transportation from the airport to the ship. Another charge is one that is entirely up to you. It is the transfer fee. This is the fee the cruise line charges to transport you from the airport to the ship. Depending on how far the ship is from the airport, will determine the fee. I have always used this hassle free mode of transportation. Some swear by finding a cab and paying to go to the ship when they arrive, but I have always taken the transfer fee option. It is just one more item that can be hassle free and you know the cruise line's transportation will make it to the ship. You also know the cost of the transportation if booking the cruise line's transfers, unlike waiting to find a taxi and possibly paying more. Currently, with the economy reeling from high gas prices, cruise lines have added a fuel surcharge, much like the airlines. It is usually a per person per day fee and has become a part of doing business as cruise lines use large quantities of fuel to take us to great locations on our vacation. All cruise lines vary in their charge, so you can check with your agent for the current charge. Another option to consider that is not part of your cruise fare is travel insurance. This is not required and if you are considering travel insurance, you do not have to purchase the cruise line's travel insurance. This insurance varies from cruise line and from insurance company, but it is for your peace of mind if you have to cancel your trip or have a delay in your trip. There are many companies on the internet that offer this and your agent can recommend several that they have experience in using. Again, for minimizing the amount of work involved in booking, purchase the cruise line's insurance for added peace of mind. After considering all your options and added fees (taxes, port charges, transfers), if the price is within your budget, all you have to do now is book your cruise vacation. Your agent will ask you to make a cabin selection. You should have discussed this already, but once the commitment to book is made you can now select your cabin number or select best available, whereby the cruise line will choose the cabin for you at a later date. You will be asked to make a deposit on your cruise. This deposit is roughly $500.00. You may be required to pay more depending on how close to the booking date you are, but if booked far enough in advance, this deposit is usually enough. Approximately three months (depending on cruise line) before your departure date, you will have to pay the balance. Your agent can set up a monthly payment plan if that works better for you, but check with your agent first.

Well, now you're booked. Now what? Just wait? Nope! With the advanced upgrades to the cruise line reservation systems, you can now pre-register for your cruise on the cruise line's website. All you will need to pre-register is your booking number (received once you make your deposit), your sail date, and the name of your ship. Once you have this, log on to the cruise line's website and pre-register. You can do this anytime before your cruise at your convenience. Some lines have a cut off from one day to 2 weeks before the cruise in which you can pre-register. I like to do this soon after I book as I am still in the booking and planning mode. All cruise lines are different in the forms you fill out, but doing this online makes the boarding process on the day of your cruise so much faster and easier. After entering all pertinent information and saving the information, you will be able to log on any time and make changes if necessary. Once you are finished, some cruise lines prompt you to print out a boarding pass to make your registration process easier on the day of your cruise.

Another online feature allows you to choose your shore tours when going ashore from the comfort of your own home. This has made the cruising experience so much more enjoyable and stress free. In the past, you had to book your shore tours onboard the ship. This was a little chaotic at times. When you boarded the ship and reached your cabin, a list of shore tours and their description was waiting for you. You then had to read through all of the tours, decide on which ones you wanted to experience, and then stand in line at the shore tours desk to book the tour. That was no way to spend your vacation. The cruise lines caught on to this, so most of them started offering interactive television in your cabin where you could book your tours on the television instead of standing in line - as long as the interactive channel was working. The cruise lines have now honed their technology and you can select your shore tours on the cruise line's website from the comfort of home. This allows you a little more time in your decision process and allows you to spend more time reviewing your options. Once you book your shore tours, some cruise lines will charge your credit card as soon as you book, while others will not charge you until you board the ship.

Once you have pre-registered and booked your shore tours, you can sit back and wait. You now just have to make your final payment and in the meantime tell all your friends and family about your upcoming cruise vacation. Approximately 30–45 days prior to your departure, you will receive a packet in the mail from your cruise line. It will have all your travel documents needed to board the ship: a copy of your pre-registered forms, a ticket for the credit card you will use to make all your onboard purchases, your airline vouchers (if you chose the cruise line's air), your transfer vouchers (if you chose these), your cruise contract, and luggage tags. If there are any documents that need filled out, now is the time to do it - in the comfort of your home. Most cruise packets also come with a little brochure of frequently asked questions and an outline of what you can expect from your cruise vacation: dining options, attire, what is included in the price of your cruise, weather, itinerary, etc. You will want to verify that all of the information is correct, and if not, contact your agent immediately.

All that is left is for you to pack your luggage, arrive at the ship on time (whether flying or driving), check-in at the cruise terminal, board the ship and ENJOY!!! Make sure you leave your family and friends the name of your ship and itinerary before you leave, just in case. Also, leave them the cruise line's phone number which, if not in your boarding documents, will be on the cruise line's web site.

CHAPTER 5

ARRIVING AND BOARDING FOR YOUR CRUISE

Let's now make sure you are prepared for the boarding process. When you arrive, don't be too early. What is too early? Well, it all depends on the size of the ship and the port of embarkation (where you will board and depart). Unlike a hotel, where guests arrive and leave at different times of the day and different days of the week, a cruise ship has all guests arriving on the same day, all staying for the same length of time. That means all guests will be leaving the same day and all in a relatively short period of time. The larger the ship, the more passengers trying to embark on the first day and the more trying to disembark on the last day, in a relatively short period of time. We will discuss in a later chapter leaving the ship the final day, but the ship needs to be able to clear all guests through customs and have all guests ashore by a certain time so they can "turn around" the ship: cleaning rooms, setting up accounts, loading food and beverages, etc. If you are flying in on the day of your cruise, you usually don't have an issue as most flights are going to put you at the airport late enough in the morning. If you fly in a day early, you will want to arrive at the port close to boarding time on the day of your cruise. The documents you receive from the cruise line will list the boarding time for your port of departure. Arriving a day early and spending a relaxing day at a hotel is recommended. You want your cruise vacation (as any vacation) to have as few complications as possible. Airline delays, cancellations, rebooking, over-bookings, etc could potentially result in you missing the ship. High fuel costs cause airlines to cut flights and cancel routes in order to remain profitable, all of which cause headaches. Weather delays can also cause havoc on your vacation. Letting the cruise line book your air helps in alleviating some of the headache, but the ship will still sail on time. Unlike a hotel that will be available if you are delayed (as long as you call them and update your arrival), a cruise ship has a schedule to maintain and will leave on time. Depending on where you live, direct flights may not be an option and your air itinerary will involve connections; the more connections, the more delays likely. A good rule of thumb, though, is to book the earliest flights available. The earlier in the morning, the better chance those delays at the airports have yet to begin. If you are delayed, inform the airline agents, so they can try and accommodate you on the next flight if necessary. At the same time, call your cruise line and inform them of the delay. So, back to the main point, arriving a day early is a great idea and the hotel price for that extra night will be worth the peace of mind of being at your destination in plenty of time. The added bonus of arriving a day early is that your vacation has begun a day early and you can explore the island or city where your ship will be leaving. If arriving a day early, the morning of your departure, enjoy a leisurely breakfast at the hotel and relax while all the passengers disembark the ship after enjoying their cruise vacation, then when it is time (don't forget to check the brochure for boarding times, or call the cruise line if unsure) have the hotel take you to the ship.

If you are driving to the ship, there is parking available near the pier, although some ports have limited space while others have more space than others. Again, allow yourself plenty of time if driving on the day you are to depart. You never know when you may have to change a tire or wait in traffic or have construction delays. If arriving a day early -great, otherwise plan your driving route well and take a map in case you have to find an alternative route. In this instance, you may arrive at the pier early just to make sure you arrive on time. The only thing that will happen if you arrive early is that you will have to wait, either in line or in a lounge in the cruise terminal. The cruise lines will not let you board before all passengers have exited and the ship has been cleared. A good rule of thumb is to arrive by noon on the day of embarkation.

If you have arrived by air on the day of your cruise, you will first collect your luggage. Remember, you should already have the cruise line luggage tags attached to your bags. In the baggage claim area, you will find a representative for your cruise line. If this is a port where there are many cruise lines sailing, you will see all the various cruise line reps in the baggage area. They will have uniforms for their respective cruise line and a clipboard and sign identifying them. You will want to check-in with a rep from your cruise line. What if there is more than one ship sailing that day for the same cruise line? The cruise line rep will check you in and keep passengers for each ship separate, and your luggage tag will likely be different from another ship of the same cruise line. This is not always the case as each cruise line has its own system, but make sure you have your luggage tags on your bags. Once you claim your luggage, you will meet where the representative informed you to gather. Once everyone has their luggage and everyone has checked in, make sure you have your transfer voucher in hand if you purchased one. The agent will help you find this voucher in your cruise packet. Once the bus arrives, everyone will be conga-lined to the waiting bus. This is where things differ among cruise lines. On some cruise lines, you will take your luggage to the bus. Once everyone has boarded and the bus driver has loaded the entire luggage, you will proceed to the ship. Other cruise lines have you drop off your luggage at a nearby waiting delivery truck near your bus. You will hand over your luggage and they will load it onto the truck and once the truck is full (long after you have boarded) they will deliver your luggage to the ship. Make sure you have all needed medicines, all needed documents, and anything else you will need with you in a carry-on as it will be several hours before you see your luggage again. The bus will transport you to the pier and your ship. If your luggage came with you on the bus, you will not be able to get off the bus at the pier until the driver has unloaded the luggage. Once he has done this, you will depart the bus and gather your luggage, making sure you have it all. Once you have checked for your luggage, you will inform the luggage handlers on the pier that you have all pieces verified and they will load the luggage into containers which will eventually be loaded onto the ship. Again, make sure you have everything with you that you will need before proceeding to the terminal, as it will be several hours before you see your luggage. Now, if you arrived by car or a day early and are arriving at the ship from the hotel, you will drop off your luggage with the ship's personnel and they will load the luggage as stated above.

No matter what mode of transportation you used to reach this point on the pier, you will have to enter the terminal to be processed so you can board your ship. You will enter the building making sure you have your cruise documents in hand. You will eventually pass through the x-ray machine and the metal detector. I have arrived at different times of the day and have not found any particular time that is always the best time to avoid waiting in line. I have waited for 45 minutes and I have walked through in less than 10 minutes. If you arrive early, before everyone has disembarked (and some do arrive bright and early), you will have to wait until everyone is off the ship before they begin the boarding process. There is no set amount of time that you can expect to wait. It just depends on traffic flow and how quickly the cruise agents can process the forms. Remember, earlier I stated that once you book, you should go on line and pre-register? You remember I stated that once your cruise packet arrives you should fill out any necessary forms and call if there are any errors? This is where being proactive pays off. As cruise lines expand their websites to allow more documents to be filled out in advance, the need to fill out pages of forms at the check-in counter has been eliminated. I would suspect at some point in the future, all you will need is a boarding pass much like the airlines and embarkation will become much easier and faster. You will see people cumbersomely filling out the documents on the plane or in line in the cruise terminal trying to find a pen and something to write on before they get to the check-in counter. Don't be one of them, especially if there is no line. Again, cruise lines are making it easier than ever before to have all this completed in advance of your arrival. Since you have yours filled out, the amount of time you spend with the agent at the counter will be minimal. Once all your documents are verified you will need to set up your onboard charge account with the agent. Most people use a credit card. You can use cash or travelers checks, but a credit card is much easier. Once this is done, the cabin key you receive (it is actually a card) will be your onboard charge card (as no cash or credit cards are used onboard) and your key to enter your cabin. Your cabin key will either be handed to you at the counter or you will proceed to another area where you will collect your key, or card, as it is a card. Once you have your key, you are on your way to boarding the ship. Before you board the ship, you will pass a photographer taking pictures of arriving passengers. This will not be the last time you see someone snapping photos as the ship's photographers are everywhere. Just as you enter the ship's lobby, you will be greeted and directed to have your new cabin card/charge card activated with your picture. You just insert your card into a slot, smile for ship's security and retrieve your card and enter the ship. This card will not only be used for your cabin and as a charge card for your onboard purchases, but it will also be used every time you leave and return to the ship. You will drop your card into the slot when going ashore, and will do the same when you re-board. The ship's security staff will match you with your picture and this allows them to know who is ashore and who is onboard. Once you pass this area, you have arrived and your vacation begins.

CHAPTER 6

ALL ABOARD

Now you are onboard looking around and wondering where do I go? If you arrive before 1pm, your cabin may not be ready yet. In this case, you will be directed to the lunch buffet on deck at the top of the ship. Otherwise, you can head off to your cabin and check out your new home. Once you board, someone will be handing out a pocket-sized fold-out showing the ship's deck plan so you will have your own map to use to get lost, but the ship's crew will be able to help you find your way around the ship. After you find the buffet and enjoy lunch, explore the ship. Some ships offer a guided tour with one of the ship's staff. This is a nice option as you will get to see all the highlights of the ship and explore without getting lost - this time. This is a nice familiarization tour and you can inquire once onboard. If you like to "go it" on your own, this is a fun way to find your way around and see a lot of the ship before everyone is onboard trying to do the same thing.

If you are able to go to your cabin, check out the daily newsletter that will be waiting for you in your cabin. It will list daily activities and upcoming events. You can check off the items you want to do and even make reservations if you plan on dining in one of the specialty restaurants, if you plan on a massage or manicure, or if you plan on having your hair done for a special evening. If you haven't already booked shore tours, now would be a good time to look at the tours available and make your reservations. Your newsletter (named differently for each cruise line) will be waiting for you each evening (for the next day's events) after your cabin steward has turned down your bed. At some point, between now and the safety drill, you will have the opportunity to meet your cabin steward. He will introduce himself and let you know he will be taking care of you for the rest of your cruise. If you require anything for your cabin, he will be the person to help you. If you have any special requests or needs, now is the time to discuss these issues. If he can help you he will, if not, he will inform you who to contact. If your luggage has not yet arrived go and explore. If your luggage does arrive before you set sail, haul it in your cabin and go explore. You don't want to miss the ship's sail away on deck because you were unpacking your clothes. They can wait until a later time. I always enjoy watching the ship's lines being pulled in and the ship maneuvering its way away from the pier and out of the harbor.

Before the lines are pulled in and the ship sails away, there is an event that all must attend - the mandatory life boat drill. Before the drill, there will be many announcements preparing you for the upcoming event. You will be directed to your cabin to put on your life jacket and proceed to your muster station. The muster station is the area that you will gather before boarding the lifeboats in the event there is an emergency. On the back of the door of your cabin you will see a map as to where you are to go and where your muster station is located. The ship is divided into many muster stations. Once you arrive at your muster station, you will be directed by ship's crew on how to proceed to the lifeboats in the event of a real emergency. The life boat drill is handled differently by each cruise line and the time involved is also different, but it is for your safety so listen carefully. Do not even think of hiding out in your cabin, as all cabins will be checked to ensure everyone attends. Once the life boat drill begins, you know two things: one is that everyone is aboard and two that your cruise vacation is moments away. After the life boat drill is over, you can head up on deck for the sail away party and begin your cruise vacation.

Information regarding your dining assignment will also be in your cabin if not presented to you at registration. If you have assigned dining, you are not obligated to dine in the same place every night. While the dining room, dining time, and table are assigned to you, you can eat at the specialty restaurants if you choose or if you had a busy day at sea or in port and you don't feel like dinner in the main dining room, you can eat at the buffet, the pizzeria, or you can order room service. All dining venues, dining times, and attire recommendations will be listed in your daily newsletter. If you decide you are unhappy with your dining assignment and would like a change, you will need to see the maitre d' to request a change. The dining experience has come a long way and if you are worried about the food being high caloric and fattening, you have many options. Healthy eating choices are one of the cruise line's hottest trends as cruise lines offer many choices and dining options. You can eat pizza and ice cream and rich desserts the entire cruise, you can try and eat your money's worth for the cruise, you can sample everything the line has to offer (not sure if that is even possible as there is so much), or you can eat sensibly and you can eat healthy. Dining room menus have at least one choice for each course that you can choose to maintain a healthy eating lifestyle. Gaining weight, losing weight, or maintaining weight is up to you. You are on vacation, and a lot of us do tend to take liberties with our food and drink consumption and our lifestyle. Don't be worried that you won't get enough to eat or will not be able to eat healthy. There are more and more options for eating healthy on cruise ships and they are very delicious. You know, you can always work off that extra dessert on the treadmill or jogging track. If you have special dietary needs most cruise lines will accommodate your needs. You will want to discuss this with the cruise line about a month or two months before your departure date. This will give the cruise line time to meet your necessary needs. If you are on a low sodium or low fat diet, this can be accommodated after you board, but it is still wise to contact your cruise/travel agent and the cruise line to ensure you will be satisfied with your request.

If you are planning a special event or celebrating a special occasion, you can pre-book some of these big events online or with your agent or directly with the cruise line. You can pre-reserve a drink package, honeymoon package, birthday celebration, sail away package, or a wedding/

anniversary package. You can even be married or have your vows renewed. You can have your room decorated; you can have a cake, appetizers, and champagne or wine for your celebration. You will want to decide early if you want to purchase a package and book early enough to allow the cruise line plenty of time to accommodate your request. If you pre-arranged any of these services, you will have confirmation waiting for you in your cabin when you arrive.

You are aboard and your vacation awaits you. You can do whatever you would like to do. You can do as much or as little as you prefer, it is your vacation.

CHAPTER 7

WHAT TO DO ON YOUR CRUISE

Well, you are aboard and sailing to your first port of call and if you have looked at your daily newsletter and still wonder if you will be bored on the ship or on shore, ask some fellow cruise passengers. Some enjoy a cruise of sun and sea and relaxation with a book on the beach or by the pool on the ship. Others will be participating in pool activities, trivia games, cruise ship Survivor or hanging ten surfing on the ship. If trying to surf in front of fellow passengers is not your thing, you can always surf the internet as cruise ships offer internet cafes for their guests. I am no expert as to the extent of these services as I do not need to stay in contact during vacation or need to surf the net. I have used the service a couple of times to print boarding passes for my return flight or a parking coupon where I parked my car. That is the extent of my use of the internet cafes.

Internet fees are per minute fees, but if you need to stay in touch you can purchase a package with bundled minutes that would be much cheaper than paying for every minute you use each time you log on. If you need to stay in touch, you can also use your cell phone. You will see a lot of passengers using them, even if it is to just call home and brag about the vacation. Cruise ships are becoming more cell phone friendly as new services are being explored. Check with your cruise line and cell phone provider to see what and where coverage will be available and what your rates will be for your itinerary. You can even bring your computer for your need to stay in touch. Some of the newer ships have internet connection in the cabins and others are totally wi-fi. You are more than welcome to use the phone in your cabin, but the per-minute rates are extremely high. When you consider spending $6 per minute for your cabin phone or roaming fee on your cell phone, you can quickly see the cell phone would be best. Even if your cell phone does not work on the ship, you should be able to receive service once on shore. If staying connected is important when on vacation, you will want to investigate with your agent, before you book, which ships have the service you require. If you are traveling with children or a group of family members or friends, it is not a bad idea to bring cell phones that you can use as radios or you can bring walkie-talkies to keep track of family members or friends. It is a great way to keep track of where everyone is on the ship.

If you enjoy gambling, the casinos on cruise ships are getting larger and larger. You can enjoy slots, black jack, Caribbean poker, and other table games. You can join black jack tournaments and slots tournaments. Casinos are only open once the ship is at sea. It is not a bad idea to set your spending limit before you board the ship, or at least before you enter the casino. As the ever popular BINGO is a part of gambling, you will be able to find several games played each day. As the cruise progresses the jackpots get bigger and on some lines the grand game prize is winning a free cruise! There are a lot of entertainment venues that do not require spending money, or gambling money. You can attend the game shows that the cruise lines offer, you can participate in trivia games, you can enjoy a Vegas style show, and you can enjoy pre-dinner music at the piano bar or in one of the many lounges throughout the ship. Your daily bulletin will list all the activities and their locations that are planned for the day.

On sea days, the ship's activities will be varied and plenty. You definitely have the option of lounging by the pool with a nice cold beverage and enjoying the sights and sounds; or you can participate in a number of activities offered for your enjoyment. You can ride a merry-go-round or try a zip line while onboard. You can learn to scuba. You can attend an onboard art auction with complimentary champagne. Do not worry about how you are going to get the piece in your luggage. You will be able to ship all of your art pieces home. You can attend a movie in a movie theater on some ships or watch a movie on the outdoor big screen on other ships. You can play bingo, watch a game show, watch a glass blowing demonstration, attend a cooking demonstration, or you can make your own pottery and take home your artwork. You can participate in a wine tasting. You can play bridge. You can even go to the spa and have a manicure, pedicure, massage, and have your hair cut and styled (the entire spa features are at an additional fee). If planning on going to the spa, reservations are required and fill up very fast. If you are more active, you can play basketball, go bowling, play pool volleyball, play tennis, you can work out in the fitness center, or you can cool off in the pool or water slide. Some ships are now creating water parks for you to enjoy, whether getting wet or just people watching. You can learn to surf on some ships and on certain ships you can ice skate, or learn to ice skate. You can test your prowess at rock climbing or you can bungee trampoline jump. And you can eat and shop, not necessarily in that order. The ship's gift shops will be open while at sea, so you can purchase t-shirts, last minute forgotten items, perfume, jewelry, and duty free liquor. You may want to take time and attend one of the shore talks about upcoming ports of call. There are also shopping lectures to help you maximize your time in port and to visit the various stores recommended by the cruise lines. Again, you have the option of doing absolutely nothing, if you so desire.

Night life onboard the ship takes on a little different vibe. Dinner is a special event. If you have assigned dining or you decide to eat at a specialty restaurant, you will definitely enjoy a multi-course meal with exceptional service. Usually, two nights are formal nights in which men wear suits and ladies wear dresses. You will still see men in tuxedos and women in gowns, but depending on which cruise line you are sailing, it is not necessary. The other nights are casual and on these nights the men wear golf shirts and pants (not jeans) and the women wear dresses, pant suits or something a little less casual than on formal nights. I am definitely not an expert on women's attire as I think more than 2 pairs of shoes is plenty and the shoe issue has resulted in some great debates while packing! The cruise packet you receive in the mail and the cruise line's brochure will help you with which type of attire is appropriate. Your daily newsletter will inform you as to the dining room mood and attire. In any case, evening dining is an event and should be experienced as it is much different than dining at home and very classy - like what could have been experienced years ago when it was customary to dress for the theater. Before dinner, you can stop off at the piano bar and enjoy a drink and listen to the music. You can relax in a lounge and listen to the onboard entertainment while enjoying a pre-dinner cocktail. After your elegant dining experience (no matter the dress code in the dining room, you will enjoy an elegant dining experience), you can continue your evening by attending a Vegas style show in the ship's lounge. You can enjoy an ice skating performance after dinner. You can also enjoy an outdoor water show with aerialists, divers, acrobats, and trapeze artists plunging into the pool as part of the show. You may listen to a band in one of the lounges or you may wish to try your hand in the casino. There are disco lounges, ball room dancing, magicians, jugglers, comedians, piano bars, or champagne bars. The lounges at the top of the ship that are laid back during the day as you enjoy great sea views, are full of lively fun and entertainment in the evening. The ship takes on a whole new life at night.

On days when the ship is in port, you can still participate in various onboard activities as some passengers are content to remain onboard and enjoy the day while not having as many fellow passengers around. Your daily newsletter will inform you of what activities are available. One thing to consider if you are planning on booking a treatment in the ship's spa, you may receive special offers to be used when the ship is in port as the spa will still be open and will want to generate money while the mass of passengers spend their day on shore. Check with the spa and check in your daily newsletter for special offers. While your ship is in port it is time to explore the islands/country/city. After all, you probably picked an itinerary for a reason, and that reason was to see the sights of a new place.

After you booked your cruise, or perhaps you waited until you boarded the ship, you looked at all the shore tours that were offered for your cruise itinerary. Whether you booked your tours at home or waited until you arrived on the ship, it is a good idea to attend the port talk lecture for each stop on your itinerary. You will receive detailed information, which will give you a good idea of what to expect. If you booked your tours at home, you will receive your shore tour tickets in your cabin either on the first day when you arrive or they will arrive that evening. If you book shore tours once you are onboard, you will receive your tickets before your first port of call. If you happened to book a shore excursion and then decided you would rather select another tour, just check in your daily newsletter for the cancellation deadline and if you are within the time frame, and space is available on your new selection, you will be able to change your tour. Popular tours fill up fast and you will discover which ones are popular if you attend the shore excursion briefings. There are a couple of different thoughts on going ashore. Those thoughts are based either on pricing or on personal preference or both.

Some passengers enjoy going off on their own. If you are planning on exploring what is next to the port or within walking distance, then you really do not need to book a shore tour and this is definitely the cheaper option. Depending on your interests, you may want to do something more involved and will need to find transportation and possibly a tour company to fulfill your need. Once you are ashore, you will find numerous taxis and plenty of tour operators willing to take you on a tour of the island, shopping, snorkeling, parasailing, etc. A lot of these will be very familiar as they are similar, if not the same to those offered onboard the ship. For the most part, these tours will be cheaper than those offered on the ship. The pricing difference varies and you will probably be able to negotiate a reasonable price. Make sure you finalize and agree on the price and what highlights are included before you start the tour.

There are some ports where the best and sometimes only option is to book your activity onboard. There are a couple of reasons for this: one could be the distance between the ship's pier and any local attractions or infrastructure; another reason could be a limited amount of shore options as some islands or cities are more limited as to what they can offer. If you are not familiar with the port or perhaps you do not speak the language of your port of call, you may opt for an organized tour with the cruise line. It will depend on your personal preference. If you have approached this cruise as one in which you are letting other people handle as much of your trip booking as possible, then let the cruise line take care of your bookings ashore. You also have added peace of mind as the organized tour you booked will take care of your transportation needs, meals (if applicable), and ensuring the ship does not leave without you. That's right! If you book a tour through the cruise line, the ship will not leave without you if your tour is delayed because of traffic or a breakdown or any other occasion that may arise. If touring with independent operators, they will do their best to get you back to the ship on time, but if something should occur to delay your return, you will not be guaranteed the ship will be waiting for you when you get back. This is a very important aspect you need to consider. Also, just because you booked a shore excursion from the ship, does not mean a guarantee the ship will wait if you decide to go on your own after the tour has ended. Sometimes, at the end of the tour, you will have the option of returning to the ship or being dropped off in town to shop or explore on your own. Once the tour is over and has returned to the pier, any sightseeing or shopping you do beyond the tour will be your choice and returning to the ship on time will be your responsibility. I, personally, like this guarantee of not being stranded on the island if something happens on your tour. On one particular cruise, we were whale watching in Alaska. As our boat was returning it developed engine problems and we were not going to make it back to the ship on time. The tour operator sent another boat. This new boat was tied up to our boat and we all precariously stepped from one boat to the next and in a short period of time we were on our way back to the ship. I never once worried about not making it back to the ship on time as we were on an organized tour from the cruise line. On another cruise, in Cozumel, Mexico, a lot of passengers enjoyed the festivities at a local bar. It is a longer walk from the bar to the ship than I thought. We made it back with time to spare, but a couple of others did not and missed the ship. They had to catch up with the ship at the next port of call - at their own expense.

On each cruise, I hear from fellow passengers how they found a driver who gave them the best tour and was wonderful and inexpensive. I, personally, have only experienced this luck once or twice. I have never heard anyone say that they took a private tour that was awful and/or expensive. Maybe when that happens, they have kept it to themselves. Once my tour is over, I usually shop around the local tour companies for pricing information for different sight-seeing tours and have discovered that the prices are not a lot less than the cruise line's prices. This is my way of affirming I made the right choice. That is not to debunk the successes of passengers that "go it" on their own. I like not having to haggle for this part of my vacation experience and I want the peace of mind of being able to make it back to the ship on time. Some of the islands/cities become very congested with traffic (human and auto) when ships are in port and delays are to be expected. Again, it is all about your peace of mind and your adventurous side.

CHAPTER 8

LAST DAY OF YOUR CRUISE

The last day of your cruise is still part of your vacation, but there are some things that will need settled and finalized in preparation for your departure the next morning (discussed in the next chapter). Within the last 2 days of your cruise, the cruise director will hold a briefing for all passengers, recommending that one member per family attends so you can understand the rules and procedures for leaving the ship on your last morning. Most of this information will be provided in the daily newsletter and cruise lines are starting to replay the briefing on your in-cabin television, continuously, once the cruise director has finished his briefing. If this is your first cruise, it is a good idea to attend and listen to the information the cruise director has to offer. I will give you an overview in this chapter, but the rules change and each cruise line is different so this is general information, but will at least give you an idea what to expect.

As with any vacation, at the start of vacation you have to pack your clothes and at the end of the vacation you have the pleasure of packing again. The concept holds true for cruises. Well, there is an exception. If you book a suite with a butler, you can opt to have your butler pack for you; but for the rest of us (the majority) we do it the old-fashioned way: ourselves. On a cruise, packing has a couple of twists that you will need to consider. First, if you participated in the fine art of shopping and delighted the local economy with your purchases, you may be wondering how you are going to get everything home. Well, I guess that concept is for another book, because this is one item you will have to creatively figure out on your own. Here are a couple of the other twists. You will receive, in your cabin, new color coded luggage tags. These will be used to organize and gather your luggage tomorrow in the ship's terminal when you leave the ship (debark or disembark). So, make sure you remove your old luggage tags that you used to arrive on your first day and replace them with the new luggage tags. These colored tags usually represent the group you will be in, the next morning, when leaving the ship. The group you are in is based on your transportation needs for your final destination home. You will also find, in your cabin, where your group will be waiting in the morning to clear the ship, based on your new luggage tags. Now, once you have everything jammed into your suitcases you need to make one last check because on your last night, you will place your luggage outside your cabin door for the crew to collect. You will not see this luggage again until morning so make sure any medications or hygiene products you will need in the morning are left out, much the same as when you handed over your luggage to airport personnel or ship personnel on your first day. Your room steward, all the room stewards, will be very busy tonight gathering the thousands of pieces of luggage and taking them to the lower levels of the ship so they can be off-loaded in the morning. Don't worry; the room stewards make more than one walk-through in the corridors. They make several trips to gather the luggage through the night and then have the chore of cleaning and disinfecting all the cabins the next morning after you leave. They are very busy during this time period. Here is the most important advice of all - do not pack the clothes you are going to wear the next day. This is what makes your last day of a cruise vacation different than a land vacation: you will not have your luggage in the morning. Not only do you want to keep medications and other essentials for the morning, but you need to make sure you have clothes (shirt, pants, underwear, socks and shoes). Along with essentials, do not pack any documents you are going to need to leave the ship (discussed soon). You will hear your cruise director tell stories about passengers who forgot to leave something out to wear the next day. Also, anything you leave out will need to fit in your carry-on the next morning.

Also waiting in your cabin along with the new luggage tags will be a Customs Declaration form. Only one member of your family has to fill out this form. The cruise director will provide you all the information you need to fill out this form in the briefing, which hopefully you attended. Your cruise itinerary will determine your customs allowances. In general, your customs allowances are $800 per person (even the kiddies) for U.S. citizens. Your cruise director will have the current allowances for the time of your cruise. If one of your ports of call is St Thomas, your allowances increase. For the most part the form is basic. You include your family name, address, passport #, places you visited, number of family members in your party, how you are returning home, and the amount you spent on purchases abroad. You will need to have this form filled out for the next morning. Fill it out today so it is one less thing to worry about when you are leaving the ship. If your purchases add up to more than the allowances, you will have to pay a tax and will do this before you leave the customs area at the cruise terminal. You can sometimes pay this onboard if you are required to present yourself to the immigration officials before leaving the ship.

In the past, immigration personnel would clear the entire ship at once when it was time for everyone to start leaving the ship. With today's heightened security, you now present yourself to an immigration official onboard the ship sometime before you leave, presenting documents of proof of your citizenship. Everyone in your family must attend and be present together. This is usually held in a lounge onboard the ship and there are usually announcements made as to when and where this will be held. Watch your daily newsletter for this information. The process does go pretty fast, but with every passenger having to go through this, the lines can become pretty long.

One other item you will find in your cabin along with the new luggage tags and Customs Declaration form is a comment card/survey. When filling this out (and it only takes a few minutes) please remain objective. Do not let one bad incident spoil your whole vacation or do not let one incident affect how you rate other areas of the ship. Here is why this is important.

The comment cards are taken very serious by the cruise lines and the staff onboard the ship. There is a great chance that your head waiter is in that current position because of the comments made on the comment cards. Cruise lines use these comments/surveys for promotion of staff and they use them for reward and recognition. Usually, the ships in the fleet compete against one another for top honors. I am not going to ask you to rate "outstanding" on every item, but if the ratings are not above "meets expectations" the cruise line and staff begins the process of determining why the item rated did not "exceed expectations". I will ask you to keep in mind that the cruise staff works very hard to make your vacation exceptional. They are working 7 days a week, twelve hour days are not uncommon, 6–8 months at a stretch and far from home and their loved ones. That is all I am going to ask of you when you are filling out the comment cards. Oh, I have had an occasion or two when a particular area was not up to par. I rated the area and I made a note in the "comments" section as to why, but I did not let that one item cloud my overall ratings or ruin my vacation. I will give you one example. On our very first cruise, I booked a balcony cabin. This was at a time when ships were just starting to be built with more balconies as this had become the new trend. I boarded the ship and was excited to learn that I had received an upgrade. Then I opened the door to my cabin. The cabin was definitely an upgrade, but I lost my balcony to floor to ceiling windows. I was not happy; this was my first cruise and I was really excited about having a balcony. Naturally, the ship was completely booked and I could not change cabins, but I did voice my appreciation of the cruise line's good will in providing me an upgrade; unfortunately, it upgraded us out of our balcony. I did not let this ruin my cruise (it just made me envious of those with a balcony), nor did I allow it to determine how I rated the comment card. Once I relaxed, I realized that this was a great cabin and the upgrade was a nice gesture from the cruise line. On the last night, much to my surprise, we received a certificate for 10% off our next cruise because of our disappointment. This was another nice gesture by the cruise line. On my second cruise, I opened the door to my cabin and I was greeted with a balcony. I eventually had a cabin with a balcony and did not let the one issue ruin my cruise or bias my ratings on the comment card.

There will be another little surprise slipped under your cabin door on the last evening. It will be an itemized list of all your onboard purchases. If you did not check your account on the interactive television at least once during your cruise (you can also check your balance at the Purser's desk), you may be in for "sticker shock". All those drinks, spa treatments, and gift shop purchases have a way of sneaking up on you. If you used a credit card to prepay for all of your purchases (you would have done this your first day when checking in), you do not have to worry, they will make sure your credit card company is billed. If you prepaid with a deposit of cash or travelers checks, you will need to go to the Purser's desk and settle your account. Your cruise director may tell you that some of your fellow passenger's bills will not fit under the door, so they will knock on your door, leave the bill, and run before you open the door. I have been fortunate to not have that worry, but I have seen some that look like a phone book - many, many pages. All in having a good time! Make sure you do look this over when you receive it, not to be shocked, but to ensure that all the charges are yours and nothing outrageous sticks out. If you feel something is in error, contact the Purser's desk. From experience, let me tell you that you may not receive a refund before you leave the ship. Think about how many passengers there are on your ship. Now think about your bill. There is a paper receipt for every item on your bill. If you imagine every passenger having as many as you or even 5 or 10 paper receipts, that is a lot of paper to look through for the ship's staff to sort to find their copy of your bill. By accident, our table mate's champagne purchase was charged to my account. As I had not ordered any champagne, this charge stuck out on my bill. I disputed the claim. The cruise line searched for their copy and found the signature was not mine and refunded my credit card. This refund did not happen on the last day when it was discovered, but happened a week after I returned home. I was impressed with the time frame. A passenger in line in front of me was livid that a credit could not be handled that morning and was very unruly, and in my opinion, out of line. He had not taken the time to consider the necessary steps to investigate his claim. So, if you see something you do not think is right, the staff will investigate it for you. Another item that you may see as a charge on your bill, that you may be unaware occurs will be for gratuities.

Gratuities have been debated to extremes over the years. Here are the basics and my views. Some cruise lines do not require you to tip as they are already built into the price of the cruise. The rest of the cruise lines offer tipping guidelines for their staff and some streamline this for you. On some cruise lines, the gratuities will automatically be charged to your onboard account. One less thing you have to worry about. I like this system.

I don't have to bring extra cash for tips and I don't have to worry about saving that extra money and not accidentally spending it. If you have your gratuities charged to your account, you still have control over the amount. The cruise line will bill your account the suggested minimum. You can leave the amount as it is billed, or you can adjust the amount up or down depending on the service you received and what you determine is fair. If your cruise line does not automatically charge your account, on your last day you will receive envelopes for each staff member that you are expected to tip. You put the money in the envelope and hand the envelope to the staff member on the last evening. Here are some general guidelines. The gratuity amount varies for each cruise line, but all are close. The overall amount is around $10 per person per day. That equates to $140 for 2 people for a 7 day cruise. The breakdown averages this: room steward - $3.50 per person per day, head waiter - $3.50 per person per day, assistant waiter - $2.00 per person per day, maitre d' - $.50 per person per day. I will reiterate what I mentioned in regards to the comment cards: these people work very hard and rely on this money, so unless the service is poor (which you should address immediately with the staff member's boss), tip the recommended amount. There have been many arguments in regard to tipping and the amount to be tipped. When you look at the grand total, that is $140 added to your vacation for 2 people to cruise; but wait, you would tip your restaurant waiters a percentage of the bill if you were not on a cruise and went out to eat. You would also leave something for the hotel cleaning staff. I figure that if I were to duplicate the same elegant meal and great service at a restaurant back home, my tip for one equivalent meal and service would be more than the daily minimum for all staff members on the above list that receive a gratuity. Remember when looking over your itemized list of purchases that was conveniently left under your door, any beverage you purchase (soda, alcohol) automatically has a 15% gratuity added to your bill. When you are onboard ship, you do not have to carry cash and unlike your room steward and dining room team who you see each day, you may see a different member of the bar staff waiting on you, so the gratuity is automatically added to the bill. As far as the tipping policy and how tipping is handled, check your cruise packet that you received in the mail for specific policies.

One other item you will receive, usually before the last day, will be a small form that you fill out informing the cruise line how you will be leaving the ship. You have already filled out a similar form that you received in your packet before the cruise or perhaps you filled this out online. This information allows the cruise line to organize the passengers into groups for departing the ship on the last morning. Often the cruise line asks you to fill out a similar form on the ship to make sure they have all the information correct and can ensure your departure on the last morning is on time to meet your needs. If you do have an early flight home and want to double check that the cruise line has the correct information, stop by the Purser's desk a day or two before the cruise ends and let them know your travel plans.

This is all going to happen on your last day: the packing, the comment card, the Customs Declaration, tipping, and checking your account. You can still use your onboard charge until the last morning, so don't think that your cruise has ended. I do want to mention customs one more time. The above customs process that was described was based on the fact that your ship was returning to a port in the U.S. If you are not returning to the U.S. by cruise ship, then you will not have to declare your purchases or go through customs when your cruise has ended and you leave the ship on the last day. You will have to fill out a customs form and proceed through customs at the first airport that you will be arriving when entering the U.S. You will receive the same form and have the same information to fill out, but you will do this on the plane instead of the ship. It appears that there are a few more items to think about and to follow through when ending a cruise vacation, but there is no reason to miss and enjoy your last day. The cruise ship's activities will be like any other day and it is just another day of vacation, even if it is your last day. Since you are reading this book, you know what to expect and can plan accordingly. I always enjoy my last day the most when it is a sea day. I like to sleep in, relax on deck, and slowly and leisurely conclude those final items that need to be done before I go to bed. When I return to my cabin for the evening, I just have to throw the last couple of items in the suitcase and make sure I have not packed tomorrow's clothes.

CHAPTER 9

GOING HOME

The morning has arrived. You will not be going about your every day routine that you have grown accustomed to the last several days. Oh, you will be going ashore, but you won't be coming back onboard. Once ashore, the ship will no longer be called "home" as you will be making room for new adventurers in a few hours, but for now it is still your home and you can enjoy a few last moments. I always take one last walk around the ship in the early morning as I won't be doing that when I get home.

I know I have said this before, but every cruise line is different and so each has a little different process for your final morning. The ship arrives early in the morning while you are sleeping so that there is enough time for customs authorities to inspect the ship and luggage. Imagine how many pieces of luggage that have to be off-loaded for the inspectors to check and for the crew to organize for you to find.

Your day may begin a little early today compared to the rest of your vacation as most cruise lines will want you to vacate your cabin by 8:00 am. This allows them enough time to clean your room for the next guests. Some cruise lines now offer the option of allowing you to remain in your cabin until your group color is called, and then you can vacate your room. The cruise lines experiment with new procedures that allow them to clear the ship in time for the next arriving guests while allowing you a leisurely relaxed morning. Some of these ideas have come from the comments made on the comment cards. The color of the new colored luggage tags that you applied to your luggage last night determines where you will wait to disembark the ship. You should have received information that noted each color of luggage tag and where those with that color are to wait - usually in one of the ship's lounges. You will not be allowed to leave earlier than the time designated by your color, but you can always leave later. You can sit back and relax and have breakfast in the morning and enjoy a leisurely morning. No one can even begin to leave the ship until customs has cleared the ship. Now, if you have an early flight, you will be assigned to the color that represents one of the early groups leaving the ship. If you have a later flight or are extending your stay, take your time and avoid some of the rush. Enjoy a nice breakfast (this may be early as most cruise lines stop serving around 8:30 am), enjoy a pastry or muffin, stroll the ship, take some final pictures and relax while everyone is leaving the ship. Don't worry, everyone will leave. That little room card that you have been using when you leave and enter the ship in each port of call will be used one last time to alert the crew who is still onboard the ship. Another option if you have a late flight is enjoying one last shore excursion. Many cruise lines offer shore tours for that last morning. This is a great way to spend some time instead of sitting in an airport. You will be leaving the ship earlier, but it is one more way to extend your vacation for a few more hours. Once the time comes for you to report to your designated waiting area (based on the color of your luggage tags), make your way to the lounge or area of ship and wait for the announcement clearing your color. Some cruise lines do not make an announcement so that you can enjoy a peaceful, less hurried morning. In this instance, a cruise line staff member will come to your designated area and inform you that your group may now leave.

I like having an early flight as it is not so late when I return home, especially if I have to be back at work the next day - I try and avoid this. Overall,

I prefer to have a later flight. The morning is less rushed, more relaxed and less stressful as I know that I have plenty of time to make my flight so the little things do not bother me. I have enjoyed many shore tours the last morning before going to the airport and still had plenty of time to make my flight without being rushed. After all it is your vacation, savor every last moment. The cruise line will offer you information in regards to the shore tours offered and which ones will be available depending on your flight departure time. You will not have to worry about having enough time, as certain tours are based on ensuring you will arrive at the airport at a certain time for early flights or late flights. The cruise lines have you covered on this also. No matter what your plans are in the morning, you will leave the ship and collect your luggage.

Your luggage will be stored in a huge warehouse and organized by the color of your luggage tag. Once you make your way to this area, locate the colored area for your luggage and find your luggage. As most luggage looks alike, make sure to double check your tag to make sure it is your piece before leaving the area. There will be porters available to assist you in hauling your suitcases to your waiting transportation. Years ago, suitcases had a little pull strap with tiny wheels that flipped over with the slightest tug on the awkward short strap. Now, even the larger pieces of luggage have larger wheels with telescoping handles that make hauling your luggage around much easier. My arms no longer ache from hauling the overstuffed suitcases home. Once you have gathered your luggage, you will make your way out of the terminal. You will need to have your Customs Declaration form and ID in your hand. You will pass a customs inspector and hand over your form and ID. You generally pass two check points. One will be when you make your way off your ship before getting your luggage. Here they will check your form and ID and maybe ask a couple of questions. Once you gather your luggage, you will pass another agent and hand over your form on the way out of the terminal. This usually takes a few seconds and once cleared you are on your way home or on to your hotel or shore tour. If you booked the cruise line's transfers, you will need this voucher handy as you will be directed to the appropriate bus that will take you to the airport or hotel or shore tour.

Now that you have an idea of how the debarkation process works, I want to explain one more option in leaving the ship the next morning in regards to luggage. Most cruise lines offer an alternative to setting your luggage outside your cabin the night before, to later be collected in the terminal once you leave the ship. This service goes by different names, but I will use the name that best describes the whole process: self-assist. If you do not want to place your luggage outside your room the night before and have no desire to hunt for your luggage in the color coded terminal, you can opt for self-assist. The name is exactly that. You help yourself, no cruise members assist you. You can carry ALL of your luggage off the ship yourself. You will have the fortune of being one of the first groups off the ship, with luggage in tow. You carry your luggage off, and go through the same procedure as everyone else, except you do not have to look for your luggage in the terminal. I have never opted for this and from what I have seen, my preconceived notions have been confirmed. Hauling my luggage through the airport terminal is cumbersome at best, so hauling my luggage down stairs (the elevators will be crowded with LONG waits), down escalators, amongst hundreds of passengers, diaper bags, strollers, carry-ons strapped to the larger pieces, and souvenir bags, is not hassle free and is not an attractive alternative for me. From what I saw in the terminal and on the stairways as large groups of passengers struggle with their luggage trying not to tip the luggage and fellow passengers over, keeping the luggage organized and keeping track of the kids and their personal pieces of luggage, reinforces the phrase, "more hassle than it is worth". With all that said, there are still large numbers of passengers waiting in line to be off the ship first. That does not mean that this process will not appeal to you and it is the reason I mention this alternative to the "standard" procedure. It will depend on your preference and this does appeal to many passengers. I would like to conduct a survey as to how many passengers tried this once and then never again. I just want to be as stress and hassle free as possible on my vacation and this is too cumbersome for me.

Now that you are on your way home, you can start planning your next cruise vacation.

CHAPTER 10

THIS AND THAT

This chapter will be a reference guide to cover some topics not covered in the main portion of the book. Some of the topics will already have been mentioned in detail, but will be listed as a reminder. There is no particular order to these topics, just common subjects of interest that will keep you in the know.

Seasickness: Will you get sea sick? Well, there are no guarantees. Cruise ships are getting bigger, but you can still feel the ocean at times. Cruise ships are designed with stabilizers which are deployed to help smooth out the ride. There is a lot of calm water out there, but it will not always be calm. You can help yourself with several over the counter medications that are on the market. I recommend that you choose something that does not cause drowsiness. If you think you may become sea sick and don't think an over the counter medication will work for you, you can visit your doctor and ask for a prescription for "the patch". It is a little patch that you place behind your ear that releases medication through the skin to help with motion sickness. Another option is wristbands you can wear that work like acupuncture with pressure being applied to a certain part of your wrist. Some say if you get car sick, then you will become sea sick. I get car sick if riding in the back of the car, but I have not been sea sick on a cruise ship and I have been on many different sized ships. Take some over the counter medications with you as an insurance policy. The infirmary can dispense something for you if you do become sea sick once onboard. The question that always arises with sea sickness is "will I know I am on the ocean?" Some ships are so large you won't even realize you are on a ship, let alone on the ocean.

Safety: The Coast Guard conducts inspections of all ships that operate from a U.S. port of call making sure that the cruise lines are following all the rules and regulations that ensure the safety of passengers and crew members. Fire safety is a big concern and cruise ships have smoke detectors, sprinklers, and emergency lighting. The crew has routine training in fighting onboard fires. At the beginning of your cruise, you will go through the process of the lifeboat drill so you know what to do in case you are required to prepare to leave the ship by lifeboat.

Medical facility: There is an infirmary with an onboard doctor and nurse. These facilities are very modern and sophisticated. Some of the infirmaries are linked to a hospital in the states so the doctor onboard can have direct interaction with medical experts on land. Commonly used medication is available onboard and if you need the services of the infirmary, there will be a fee that you will have to pay. You will have to settle with your insurance company when you return home. If you become sea sick, visit the infirmary and they will provide you with medicine to help you continue your cruise.

Laundry: You can wash your own clothes in the onboard laundromat, or for a higher fee, you can have the ship launder your clothes. The laundromat is a great service if you are on a long voyage as you can pack fewer clothes and launder as you need. You could also pay to have your clothes laundered by the ship personnel. The price varies according to cruise line. Some are reasonable and some are extremely high. I have no desire to do laundry on vacation, but I also do not like to carry home dirty clothes. The laundromats are reasonably priced and again very useful for a long cruise. I usually let the cruise line clean my clothes, for a fee of course. If you pack enough clothes and don't mind carrying home dirty clothes, this is a service that you will not have to use.

Worship service: Some cruise lines offer weekly services and others only offer during certain times of year. If this is something that is a requirement for you, check with the cruise line for availability before booking your cruise.

Pregnant passengers: You definitely want to check with your cruise line as to the cut-off date for travel. Cruise lines are changing this rule again and it is now around the 24th week that is the cutoff. You do not want to be turned away at the pier, so please inform your agent and the cruise line to make sure you will be within their guidelines.

Beverages: Your cruise price will include your meals. If you decide to eat at a specialty restaurant, there will be a nominal fee. Beer and cocktails and wine and champagne are not free. You will pay for these and remember that a 15% gratuity will automatically be added to your bill. Cocktail prices aren't out of line in pricing and are comparable to being at a resort. If you want a large icy drink and a souvenir glass, you will pay a little more. As for beer, I am not a beer drinker, but if I had to judge by the amount of beer I see being sold, I will venture that it is not overly priced. There are drink specials every day and one of the bars usually has a happy hour drink special. If you are a soda drinker you will have to pay for this also. If you drink a lot of soda, you can purchase a soda card at the beginning of the cruise (about $20) and that card will cover all your soda purchases. This is great if you are traveling with kids. Iced tea, water, juice, lemonade, coffee and tea are free.

Norovirus: This outbreak always makes headlines for the cruise industry. Norovirus is NOT a cruise ship disease. Outbreaks often occur in closed or semi-closed communities where the virus can spread fast such as dormitories, nursing homes, hotels, restaurants, hospitals, prisons, and cruise ships. Unfortunately, the virus is more associated with cruise ships as health officials have to keep track of illnesses on cruise ships as opposed to resorts and hotels, so the virus is reported quicker for cruise ships. Norovirus can be passed from contaminated food or water or from one person to the next. On cruise ships, a likely source of contamination is contact with someone who is contaminated or touching the surface of something that has been infected and then touching your mouth or eyes or nose. Think about touching a surface for instance. We walk down stairs using the rail, go to the buffet and grab a sandwich and unknowingly we could be contaminating ourselves if the railing was touched by a contaminated person, and this does not have to occur on a cruise ship. You can touch something at your work place and infect yourself. Some common symptoms are vomiting, diarrhea, and stomach cramps. Not to diminish the seriousness of this disease, but I often wonder, after eating such rich foods and gorging so much on all the free food, how often these symptoms are dismissed by passengers. Cruise lines disinfect the ships not only after an outbreak, but on a routine basis. Cruise lines have hand sanitizing stations when entering the dining rooms or buffet area. Usually a crew member is present to offer you the hand sanitizer. This is one step cruise lines have taken to prevent an outbreak and a great procedure. You can contract the "stomach flu" (although this is not a flu) almost anywhere, but with the increased human contact on a ship and the quick reporting guidelines for cruise ships, it appears that this only happens on cruise ships, which is not true. As we were told to always wash our hands when growing up, that same advice applies here.

Visitors: You can have visitors at the pier, but they will not be allowed on the ship. At the start, end, or during your cruise, all friends and family members are welcome at the port facility, but because of security reasons no one will be allowed onboard. We were watching our ship prepare to leave one day and docked next to us was a sister ship. The two ships were twins with the only difference being the name. We watched a lady board our ship and decided she must be the last one to board. A few minutes later she walked down the gangway, crossed the dock, and boarded the other ship. She was a passenger, just not on our ship and was not allowed to board.

Onboard card: Your room key/card is also your charge card for onboard purchases and your "pass" to going ashore and returning to the ship. Like the lady above, without your card you will not be able to board and even if you have your card, it will not work on any other ship. You will be given this card upon check-in, you will have your onboard purchases assigned to this card, and you will have your picture taken to be associated with this card. You will need this card when going ashore. You will insert your card into security's machine to let them know you will not be onboard. You will use it for security to return to the ship via the security checkpoint where it will match the card with your picture and the correct ship. This allows ship's security to know who is onboard and who has yet to return.

Cabins: The cabin that you chose comes with some standard features. A bed of course, but you will have a safe in your cabin in which you can secure any valuables or documents you will not need until you return home. Most cabins have 110 volt AC outlet. The newer ships come with hairdryers, but to be safe, double check before you leave the house. Not all cabins have alarm clocks, so it is a good idea to bring one with you. You can use the phone to leave a wake-up call, but for insurance, bring a travel alarm. Also, your cabin will have life vests and if they do not, alert your cabin steward. As you will be attending a life boat drill early in your cruise, you will know if you are supplied with the correct number of life vests.

Brochure: It is a good idea to check out several brochures when deciding on a cruise. Not only do these brochures provide itinerary information, some have a brief preview of shore excursions. In the back of the brochures are lists of common concerns for the cruise traveler that will be a good reference guide in planning your cruise.

Shore excursions: As mentioned previously, some of the cruise line's brochures give you an overview of some of the shore tours offered for each port of call. This is nice to have when determining your itinerary. You can also go online and check out the websites for your ports of call. You can research local attractions, local maps, and you can look at the local calendar of events to see if there is an event you may like to attend. You can even go online to some cruise websites and read information or blogs about certain shore tours. I usually rely on fellow passengers on my cruise for critiques as you can find as many negative reviews as positive reviews for your interests on the web sites.

Credit cards/cash: Most places take credit cards for your purchases. Local vendors often accept cash only. The Purser's desk will cash travelers checks. I always bring two credit cards with me just in case one of them decides not to work at the moment I am buying something. A tip I received from a fellow cruiser that I have never thought to practice is notifying your credit card company where you will be traveling. If you start making purchases from a part of the world that you don't normally travel to in your everyday life, your credit card company may become suspicious and put a hold on your card. I have never done this or thought of this before, but now that I am aware of this, I may notify my credit card company before my next vacation.

Tendering: If ships are too large to dock at the port of call or there are no docking facilities, the passengers will have to be tendered ashore. Small boats from shore will come alongside your ship and transport you to the pier. The same occurs when you want to return to the ship. This is not as convenient as docking right on the pier and walking off the ship, but the cruise lines have streamlined this process over the years. Some cruise lines are creating docking facilities at some of the ports of call to eliminate the tendering process.

Sundry items: If you forgot to pack an item or ran out of something, there is a store onboard that carries a few of the most commonly used items. If you need batteries or film, the photo department can help you with this. You can purchase disposable underwater cameras for that last minute snorkeling adventure.

Travel Insurance: This can be purchased at the time you book your cruise with the cruise line or you can purchase your own travel insurance. Not everyone opts for this as it is an added cost to your vacation. As I stated earlier, a hotel will still be at the same address if you are delayed; a cruise ship has a schedule to keep and will leave on time. If you are traveling during hurricane season (June - November), your travel plans could be interrupted and altered if a storm decides to interfere with your vacation. If you are like me and live where ice and snow are part of your winter environment, then insurance may not be a bad idea as a winter storm can ground or delay your flight and wreak havoc on your travel schedule. The choice is yours and for the most part (as with many insurances) you will not need to activate your policy, but the one time you may have to, it is great peace of mind.

Passport: Most people know that traveling outside of the U.S. requires a passport. The Caribbean is the enigma. There have been several deadlines that require all travelers traveling outside the U.S. to have a passport. The rules and amendments keep changing, so the best rule of thumb is to have a passport, even when traveling to the Caribbean. Eventually, a passport will be needed for all travel and once you have one, it is valid for 10 years and once in your possession you can travel wherever you want at a moment's notice. Double check with your cruise line or your agent before you book your cruise.

TSA rules: The TSA have changed the rules several times based on security issues as to what you can carry on board a plane. Obtain a current list from the government's website so you will know how to pack and what to pack and avoid any delays while passing through airport security. I print one for each vacation, just in case something has changed since my last vacation.

VIP/Past guests: Once you sail a second time on the same cruise line, you become a repeat passenger and will be invited to a cocktail reception for all repeat passengers. As you take more cruises with the same cruise line, you will advance through different levels of VIP membership. Each level you achieve will garner you different perks for your continued cruising. Each line has a different program with different qualifications to reach each level. Some of the enhancements you may enjoy could be priority embarkation and debarkation, behind the scenes tours, discount coupons, booking discounts, and upgrades. The cruise lines recognize their past guests and show their appreciation with different services provided.

Itinerary: There is some fine print in your cruise brochure and the cruise packet that arrives in the mail before you leave for your cruise. That fine print states that the cruise line may change or substitute the itinerary to protect the safety of the guests. Hurricanes can alter the course the cruise ship takes and it may be necessary to alter the itinerary. Unfortunately, some people miss this or forget this and become quite incensed when their cruise ship has to alter course for any number of reasons. I just wanted you to be aware that there is a chance, due to unforeseen circumstances, that this could happen.

Smoking: The dining rooms and show lounges are non smoking. Some ships even include all public spaces as off limits to smoking. Usually the port side (left) of the ship on the outside decks is reserved for smoking, while the starboard side (right) is non-smoking. Check your brochure or you daily newsletter to determine the smoking areas.

Dress Code: Again, you will want to consult your brochure, cruise packet, and onboard daily newsletter. In general there are usually 2 formal nights (dark suit and tie for men and a dress for ladies). Other evenings are sport shirt and slacks. Day wear is resort casual. As far as dressing up for dinner, you always have the option of the buffet if you do not feel like changing clothes or dressing up for formal night. The cruise brochures do well in describing what to wear for the day and evenings depending on your length of cruise.

Food: You can eat 24 hours a day when you include room service and some of the ships with 24 hour pizzerias. The main dining room is open for breakfast, lunch, and the popular dinner experience. You can always eat at the buffet. There are also specialty restaurants for your dining pleasure. You can eat at a deli, or at a Chinese or Italian station, you can eat at a seafood venue, or you can eat at the grill. Try them all for an overall amazing dining experience.

Family Friendly: There are many cruise lines that cater to children and family. You will have to discuss your expectations with your agent. During the summer months and holiday seasons, cruise lines that are not known for their extensive children's program will expand their services for the traveling families during these seasons.

Comment Card: You will receive this at the end of your voyage. Fill it out and drop it off. The cruise lines depend on these ratings and comments to further enhance the cruise experience. Please, do not let one bad incident spoil your whole cruise and affect your ratings.

Shopping: The sport of shopping is everywhere. You can shop at stores onboard. I have found many great and affordable pieces of jewelry. This is how my wife is sneaky. She will tell me that she is buying the jewelry. She uses her shipboard card (room card) to pay for it. Once the cruise ends I see the bill and realize that I paid for it as her card is attached to my card, which I set up as one account with one credit card for both of us when we boarded. Sneaky, but effective. Somehow I imagine I would end up paying anyway. Some of the ports of call are famous for shopping, so I consider shopping a shore excursion in some ports. If shopping is your sport, talk to your agent so you can combine shopping and a great itinerary for your cruise vacation.

Private Islands: Several cruise lines have their own islands! When your ship arrives, you have the whole island to yourself; along with all of your fellow passengers. Some cruise lines are enhancing other island ports with new piers and expanding the shore activities so these islands, although not private or owned by the cruise line, feel like a private island. Along with sea days, I really enjoy the private island experience as I sit back and relax and enjoy the laid back surroundings. Cruise lines have built the infrastructure on these islands and as they become more popular, they keep upgrading them and they are really a highlight of the cruise.

Luggage: The last chapter will provide you a list of items to pack in your luggage. As airlines find more ways to cover the rising cost of fuel, the luggage/baggage topic continuously changes from the size and weight to the number of bags you can have and also what you are limited to as a carry-on and its contents. Check with the airline before leaving. If you are driving to the pier then you just need to check with the cruise line, but you should have no problem with 2 pieces each. I have learned one great packing tip over the years and that is packing light. You know you will bring home souvenirs and depending on your length of cruise, packing light is the rule. I quite often wear the shirts I bought myself as souvenirs on the cruise. If you decide to forgo that advice, you may rethink it after your cruise is over.

Cruise packet/documents: These will arrive several weeks before your cruise. If you have not pre-registered online, do it now. This packet will contain luggage tags, transfer coupons, boarding pass, cruise terms, a handy "frequently asked questions" guide, and an itinerary summary. It will also include your air confirmation if you booked directly through the cruise line. Please, double check that all the information is correct, including spelling of names. If you book your own airfare, you will also need to double check that the information is correct, including name spelling.

Muster station: This is an onboard term. When you don your big orange life vest for the lifeboat drill, you will proceed to your muster station. This is the area where you will gather as a group before being directed to a lifeboat. You will want to know where this is (usually a lounge) in case it is ever needed during your cruise. It will be posted on the back of your cabin door.

Spa: Most of the services in the spa require a fee. You can use the nearby fitness center on your own and they are outfitted with the very latest and most modern equipment. You can have your hair cut or have a perm; you can have a manicure, pedicure, or a massage. There are mud and seaweed body wraps. You can treat yourself to luxury. Watch your daily newsletter for specials when the ship will be in port and most of the passengers are ashore.

Booking/Reservation/Confirmation number: When booking your cruise, ensure that you receive the cruise line's actual booking/reservation/ confirmation number and not just the number provided by the agent or website. This allows you to confirm and pre-register on the cruise line's website. You can also book your shore excursions, spa packages, and specialty dining reservations with the cruise line's booking number. In case a travel agency closes its doors, having the cruise line's booking number will allow you to maintain your reservation as the cruise line has your reservation in their system. If you only have the travel agent's booking number and the agency closes its doors, you may not have a reservation with the cruise line yet (even if you submitted your deposit to the agent) if the agent did not submit your booking information.

Final Payment: Use a major credit card to pay your deposit and final payment. If the agency or any business fails, you will have protection if you paid with a credit card. Debit cards may not be covered by this protection so check with your bank if this will be your form of payment. Once you have paid with your major credit card, review your credit card statement to ensure that the deposit or final payment was charged by the cruise line and not the travel agency. You will know that the cruise line received your money if they are listed on your credit card statement.

Diapers: Just a quick note of awareness – children in diapers are not allowed in the pools. It makes sense. The Center for Disease Control is trying to prevent illnesses on cruise ships by preventing the pools from becoming contaminated with "accidents". All pools, not just those on cruise ships, adopt the premise that diapers (and specialty diapers for swimming) are not seepage or leak proof from urine or diarrhea or any other germs. Some cruise lines do have special pools (with special filtration and disinfection) for those not toilet trained. Please keep this in mind for all your children's activities and check with your agent or cruise line when booking your cruise.

Sun block: A packing necessity. You are going to be on, in, or near water. The sun will be more intense because of reflection from the water. Also, the farther south you travel (the closer to the equator) the more intense the sun. Young or old, you will not be exempt from the sun's rays. I do think that a nice tan can make one look healthier. Once you have been bundled up all winter, a little color does brighten the appearance. I am not sure how healthy years of tanning/burning will look at age 70, but sun block is the key. All ages need this protection from the sun. I can sit out all day where I live and not burn real bad. In the Caribbean it does not take long to reach the same burn and takes even less time to look like a lobster. You will see fellow passengers who decided to forgo this advice and they will look shades of red not often seen. I know some cruisers who failed to apply sun screen and they spent the next day or two in their cabin. That is not how I want to spend my vacation (cruise or land). A cloudy day may offer relief from the sun's direct heat, but the clouds will not prevent you from being burned. From my own experience, by the time you realize it, it is too late. You will be sweating and probably in the water during your cruise so don't forget to REAPPLY and reapply often.

Dehydration: I am not going to pretend to be a doctor, but I do want to make you aware of this important health issue. More than likely you will be traveling somewhere warm or hot. More than likely you are going to participate in activities. You will want to drink plenty of fluids to avoid dehydration. Ship personnel will constantly remind all passengers during the cruise to take bottled water ashore. Thirst and dry mouth are early signs that your body is taking in less fluid than is going out. Water and sports drinks are your best source. Alcohol, soda, and caffeine only compound dehydration. Dehydration can lead to heat cramps, heat exhaustion (some symptoms include nausea, lightheadedness, dizziness, headache, fatigue, and more) and if left untreated, heat stroke (some symptoms include absence of sweating, rapid pulse, difficulty breathing, confusion and more). You are on vacation and having fun in the sun and perhaps being more active will be part of your daily routine. Drink plenty of water and take water with you to the beach or on any of your excursions.

CHAPTER 11

151 THINGS TO DO ONBOARD

Most people worry that they will be bored on a cruise ship, especially on sea days. The following list is a preview of the many activities that will keep you occupied and eliminate the fear of being bored. Not all of these features can be found on any one cruise ship, but a lot of the newer mega ships do contain a lot of these activities.

1. Try your adventurous side on a zip line across the open decks.

2. Be creative and make your own pottery and take it home as a souvenir.

3. Watch the art of glass blowing.

4. Try ice skating.

5. See a Vegas style show.

6. Dine at the sushi bar.

7. Take a chance at BINGO.

8. Have a private dinner on your own balcony.

9. Work off some calories in the fitness center.

10. Test your palate with wine tasting.

11. Renew your vows.

12. Take a ride on the merry-go-round.

13. Like to bowl? You can on a cruise ship.

14. Cool off with a ride down the water slide.

15. Still not cooled off, have a water balloon battle.

16. Bocce ball on the lawn - yes, real grass on a cruise ship.

17. Attend an art auction.

18. Learn tricks of the trade at circus school.

19. Relax on deck and watch a beautiful sunset.

20. Attend a cooking demonstration and learn new recipes.

21. Scared of heights, you can still try the rock climbing wall.

22. Watch a water show performance - divers, trapeze, all onboard your ship.

23. Practice your golf swing with virtual golf.

24. Play miniature golf.

25. Join the ping pong tournament; you may want to practice first.

26. Shuffleboard is still played on the ship and has not gone away.

27. Laugh, while watching a late night comedian.

28. Watch a juggler perform on a moving ship.

29. Be amazed at an acrobatic show.

30. Try acupuncture.

31. Lather on the sunscreen and lie out on deck and sunbathe.

32. Get lost while exploring the ship.

33. Go to the spa and have a massage.

34. Read a good book.

35. Take piano lessons.

36. Have your hair cut or styled.

37. Enjoy a slice of pizza.

38. Eat all the ice cream you like - you're on vacation.

39. Walk barefoot in the grass.

40. Have a facial.

41. You can even have your shoes shined.

42. You can surf the net.

43. Watch a movie, whether in your cabin, in the theater, or on the big screen on deck.

44. Soak in the hot tub.

45. Listen to the band.

46. Like to sing? Try karaoke.

47. Show your moves and disco the night away.

48. Have a cappuccino.

49. Shop, shop, shop.

50. Cool off with a tall tropical drink.

51. Learn towel and napkin folding.

52. Sample free liquor.

53. Sign up for a blackjack tournament.

54. Enjoy fine Italian cuisine.

55. Learn to scuba.

56. Watch a psychic.

57. Catch a wave on a surfboard.

58. Try your hand at boxing.

59. Like to drive fast? Try the race car simulator.

60. Watch an ice skating show.

61. Try your arm at the slot machines.

62. Shock your family and friends with a tattoo.

63. Have fun in the arcade.

64. Head to the martini bar and sample new martini recipes.

65. Don a heavy coat (provided) and have a drink in the ice bar.

66. A pickup game of one on one at the basketball court.

67. Enjoy happy hour!

68. Participate in the guest talent show.

69. Learn digital photography.

70. Bet a hand at poker.

71. Have a manicure.

72. Play trivia games and win a prize.

73. Another popular card game - bridge tournaments.

74. Try wii.

75. Bungee jump on a trampoline and get a bird's eye view for your jump.

76. People watch - very interesting.

77. Gorge on the midnight buffet.

78. Pose in your best for formal photos.

79. Attend the port shopping talk and learn where the best values are on shore.

80. Participate, or just watch, the men's hairy chest contest.

81. Try country line dancing.

82. Hit the pool in the belly flop contest.

83. Play volleyball.

84. Have a pedicure - to match your manicure.

85. Visit the planetarium and be amazed.

86. You can even have Botox treatments.

87. Attend a lecture (financial, history, art, etc).

88. The fine art of afternoon tea.

89. Or enjoy a pint of ale.

90. Savor butter drawn lobster tail.

91. Have Chinese for lunch from the Asian restaurant.

92. Enjoy burgers, fries, and a shake.

93. Enjoy a fine cigar.

94. Have a get together and serve canapés.

95. Learn ballroom dancing.

96. Learn how to play different casino games by attending gaming lessons.

97. Stretch out in yoga class.

98. Enjoy a pre-dinner cocktail at the piano bar.

99. Check out the hypnotist.

100. Have fish and chips for lunch or a snack.

101. Visit the library and check out a book.

102. Ride the glass elevator overlooking the sea and enjoy a ride with a great view.

103. Have your favorite omelet made to your order for breakfast.

104. Walk along the garden and enjoy the manicured landscape.

105. Take a seat at the three-deck rising bar.

106. Sit on your balcony and enjoy the view.

107. Fall asleep on a deck chair.

108. Indulge at the chocolate buffet.

109. Shoot darts.

110. Learn to carve vegetables and fruit.

111. Buy a new piece of jewelry to remember your cruise.

112. Buy souvenirs for envious friends and family back home.

113. Have cotton candy while walking along the boardwalk. Yes we are still on a ship.

114. Join in a nightly parade decked out in costumes.

115. Have a panini from the deli.

116. Email your family back home and let them know how much fun you are having.

117. If you have the energy, jog a few laps around the ship.

118. Stay in and order room service.

119. Head to the bar and enjoy a night cap before turning in.

120. Relax in the spa.

121. Attend the captain's welcome aboard cocktail party.

122. Dress up for dinner and enjoy a fine dining experience.

123. Try horse racing - cruise ship style.

124. Health conscious - enjoy healthy dining selections.

125. Play pool on self-leveling pool tables.

126. Relax in a private cabana.

127. Meet new people and make new friends.

128. Take a lot of pictures and practice taking pictures that look like postcards.

129. Have strawberries and champagne.

130. Enjoy an evening stroll on deck.

131. Play cruise ship Survivor.

132. Enjoy harp music during dinner.

133. Dine in a different restaurant each night.

134. Watch an ice carving demonstration.

135. Pilates.

136. Relax with aroma stone therapy.

137. Have a glass of milk and fresh, hot cookies.

138. Play gin or drink gin.

139. Tai chi classes.

140. Play chess or backgammon.

141. Watch the big game in the sports bar.

142. See a magic show.

143. Try the putting green.

144. Attend a jewelry seminar and learn how to choose the perfect stone.

145. Participate or watch the marriage game - very funny.

146. Tennis anyone?

147. In line skating.

148. Take a tour of the galley.

149. Try a body wrap in the spa.

150. Book your next cruise.

151. RELAX!!!

I hope you found something that interests you from this list and hope that maybe this will help alleviate the excuse for not taking a cruise - that you will be bored.

CHAPTER 12

101 THINGS TO DO ASHORE

As with the list for onboard activities, this list is definitely not comprehensive. As a matter of fact some of the activities mentioned are rather generic. Take for instance snorkeling, it may only be mentioned once or twice here, but each cruise line has several snorkel adventures at various islands and they are all a little different in the destination and the activity so you have many snorkeling options on your cruise. There may be as many as 101 snorkel adventures among all the cruise lines, so while there are 101 things listed below to do ashore, remember that there can be many variations to each one of these activities. If after reading the previous chapter, you realized that there is a lot to do onboard to prevent boredom, I think you will be equally impressed with some of the featured activities to do while you are not onboard and are on shore.

Beginner's Guide to Cruising

1. Try canopy zip line across the jungle, much different than zip lining onboard the ship.

2. Try and stay dry with parasailing.

3. Go whale watching, an amazing experience.

4. Try kite surfing. I'm not coordinated enough for this.

5. Have fresh catch of the day by going salmon fishing.

6. Play golf on one of the many golf courses available around the world.

7. Try windsurfing.

8. Snorkel the coral reefs and admire all the colors.

9. Explore ancient ruins.

10. Go beyond snorkeling and scuba dive.

11. Don't want to get wet, take a submarine dive and enjoy the wonders below the surface.

12. Simply sunbathe on the beach.

13. Enjoy a long leisurely stroll along the beach.

14. Visit a butterfly sanctuary.

15. Swim with stingrays.

16. Visit an active volcano.

17. Tour a vanilla plantation and take home real vanilla.

18. Visit a rum distillery and have a few samples.

19. Shop, shop, shop.

20. Walk around the local town and stroll the waterfront.

21. Visit a rain forest.

22. Climb a waterfalls - you will get wet this time.

23. Float down a lazy river on inner tubes.

24. Try your balance with surfing.

25. Swim with the dolphins.

26. Sightsee aboard a train.

27. Enjoy a sail around an island.

28. Visit a pineapple farm.

29. No luck fishing for salmon, watch bears catch the salmon.

30. Tour an Indian village.

31. Try your luck panning for gold.

32. Take a 4-wheel drive adventure with some off the road adventures.

33. Go deep sea fishing.

34. Climb a mountain, a little different than the rock climbing wall on the ship.

35. Don't want to swim with stingrays or dolphins, go swimming with sharks.

36. Let yourself go and take the bar hop bus tour.

37. Tour a vineyard and sample the local offerings.

38. See a glacier from above with a helicopter tour.

39. Visit a pearl farm and select your very own pearl.

40. Visit the pyramids.

41. Get up close and personal with seals.

42. Go horseback riding.

43. Kayaking.

44. How about dog sledding?

45. Take a water taxi through the canals and lagoons.

46. Visit great museums around the world.

47. Take a guided island tour.

48. Another view under the sea is helmet diving.

49. Enjoy the aroma of a nutmeg and cocoa plantation.

50. Take a glass bottom boat ride.

51. Skim along the surface with an airboat ride.

52. Ride along in a racing yacht - cup style.

53. Visit a space center.

54. Enjoy a camel ride, maybe while visiting the above mentioned pyramids.

55. Soak in hot springs.

56. Visit an ice museum - probably cold.

57. Learn about totem poles in a native village.

58. Visit pink flamingos at the salt flats.

59. Explore a lighthouse.

60. Tour antebellum homes.

61. Try water cycles.

62. Dive a ship wreck or plane wreck.

63. Sample fresh sugar cane and enjoy the fibrous sweetness.

64. View nesting bald eagles.

65. Can't catch salmon and tired of bears catching salmon, visit a salmon hatchery.

66. Now enjoy a salmon bake.

67. Visit old military forts.

68. Enjoy historical cathedrals and be amazed at the workmanship.

69. Try an eco-hike.

70. Ride a trolley and visit the local attractions.

71. Have fun at an amusement park.

72. Walk along manicured botanical gardens, which are a little larger than the ones on the ship.

73. Enjoy a picnic.

74. Watch and be amazed at cliff divers.

75. Visit and photograph penguins up close.

76. See a green monkey habitat.

77. Bird watching.

78. Visit a banana plantation, fresh bananas are best.

79. Go to a luau.

80. Jump on a sea-doo and hit some waves.

81. See a tribal dance.

82. Explore caves.

83. Try Baja racing.

84. Take an aerial tram for some great views and photo opportunities.

85. Snorkel with sea lions.

86. Tour birthplaces of the famous.

87. Rent a moped and tour the country.

88. Go to an observatory.

89. Visit a turtle farm and adopt a turtle.

90. Learn about lost civilizations.

91. Ride a horse-drawn buggy.

92. Tour a mangrove habitat.

93. Attend local carnival/festival.

94. Explore a castle.

95. Visit an alligator farm.

96. See Egyptian temples.

97. Visit a nearby quiet island.

98. Watch a geyser.

99. Visit a batik studio and watch them hand make cloth.

100. Visit a civil war battlefield.

101. Enjoy a relaxing beach barbeque.

As you can see, there is a little something for everyone from the rugged adventurous activities to those that are more sedate and relaxed. Do what interests you and do not worry about trying them all, those that you want to do and do not have time will be waiting for you on your next cruise.

CHAPTER 13

101 PORTS OF CALL

In this chapter you will be able to get an idea of just how extensive the places are that you can visit on a cruise. As the cruise lines expand their itineraries to give passengers more opportunities to visit the globe, they open up new markets that years ago would not have been considered for cruising. World cruises of three months or longer used to be best way to visit far lands of the world, but now there are many options with various lengths of itineraries that allow cruise passengers to explore the earth on ship without having to book a world cruise. As passenger demand persists, more and more countries are being explored by the cruise lines and the world is really at our fingertips. The list below is a varied list of cities, countries, and/or islands. If your favorite or dream destination is not listed, that does not mean it is unavailable. If it happens that your place of interest is unavailable at this time, make a note on your comment card and write a letter to the cruise lines and perhaps, one day, it will be included in an itinerary that will interest you.

1. Antigua

2. Key West

3. St. Lucia

4. Acapulco

5. Anchorage

6. Dominica

7. Iceland

8. London

9. Sweden

10. Monte Carlo

11. Nova Scotia

12. Aruba

13. Casablanca

14. Istanbul

15. Martinique

16. Cannes

17. Russia

18. Grand Cayman

19. Amsterdam

20. Bahamas

21. Norway

22. St. Thomas

23. Seattle

24. Capri

25. Montreal

26. Curacao

27. Ketchikan

28. Moorea

29. Tortola

30. Dublin

31. Mykonos

32. Guadaloupe

33. Hilo

34. Lisbon

35. Bermuda

36. Baltimore

37. Sydney

38. Ensenada

39. Skagway

40. Ocho Rios

41. Bueno Aires

42. Miami

43. Tahiti

44. Colombia

45. Puerto Vallarta

46. Trinidad

47. New Orleans

48. San Juan

49. Genoa

50. Bonaire

51. Cozumel

52. Tokyo

53. Canary Islands

54. Copenhagen

55. Kona

56. Beijing

57. St. Kitts

58. Fiji

59. Singapore

60. Montego Bay

61. Antarctica

62. Chile

63. New York

64. Venice

65. Cyprus

66. Tampa

67. Grenada

68. Vancouver

69. Galapagos Islands

70. Cabo San Lucas

71. Corfu

72. Playa Del Carmen

73. St. Maarten

74. Port Canaveral

75. Finland

76. St. John

77. Peru

78. Alexandria

79. Barbados

80. Juneau

81. Catalina Island

82. Bora Bora

83. Turks and Caicos

84. Boston

85. Portofino

86. Melbourne

87. Rotterdam

88. Sitka

89. Costa Rica

90. Ft. Lauderdale

91. Turkey

92. Barcelona

93. Mazatlan

94. Ecuador

95. Nevis

96. Southampton

97. Bangkok

98. Rio De Janeiro

99. Santorini

100. Malta

101. Belize

As you can see, the globe is represented well by the cruise lines. Maybe this chapter is where you will want to start when choosing an itinerary. You can pick some of these places and start your research from here to determine where you want to go on one of your cruises. The options are almost endless and you should be able to find a cruise to fit your vacation needs when it comes to locations to visit and length of vacation you have available. Being bored on a cruise ship or wondering what to do once ashore while visiting one of the above places should no longer be a major concern. You may now be wondering how to choose what you are going to do as there are so many options.

CHAPTER 14

PACKING LIST

Packing is not always a pleasant part of vacation. Like cleaning gutters, packing can be one of those chores you would rather put off and forget about, until it rains or until you have to leave for the airport. Below is a list of some essentials and some everyday items that can be easily overlooked. I seem to add to my packing list each year as something comes up that I wish I had brought with me and never thought to pack, until that moment when it is needed. I am sure you have your own packing list, but this may help make it complete. If you do not have one, you may use all or part of this list I have put together.

Passports

Drivers License

Health Insurance card

Credit Cards

Beginner's Guide to Cruising

Cash or travelers checks

Tip money (set aside so you do not spend)

Airline Tickets

Cruise Tickets and cruise packet

Cameras and batteries and film

Alarm Clock

Clothes - you decide what to take based on your itinerary

Suntan Lotions

Swimwear

Contacts or glasses, if required, along with saline. Check TSA list of amount allowed in carry-on

Travel iron

Books for relaxing reading or to pass the time on your flight

Sunglasses

Medication for seasickness

Aaron Mase

Hygiene items (deodorant, toothbrush, toothpaste, floss, perfume, cologne, razor, cream, aftershave)

Cold medicine

Umbrellas

Band aids

Hair dryer (check with cruise line to see if one is provided)

Curling iron

Comb, brush

Hand sanitizer

Airborne, vitamins, other supplements

Lint brush

Cell phone and charger

Room freshener

Q-tips

Tissues

Make up kit

Nail kit

Snacks - come in very handy on an airplane as the snacks are minimal and pricey

Vicks - newly added to help clear a cold and be able to breathe at night

Souvenir list

Parking coupon - if parking near the airport

TSA List of allowable items.

Small sewing kit for those lost buttons or small snag

Any medication you are required to take

Take a copy of the ship's deck plans from the brochure

Snorkel gear, if you own your own

Sneakers, shoes, sandals, water shoes

Make sure you check to see what items are allowed in your carry-on and which items are only allowed in your checked luggage. Saline for contacts is allowed in your carry-on, but only in a certain size container. Deodorant sounds simple enough, but currently gels of any kind are not allowed in your carry-on; not even gel soled shoes are allowed, so it is important to check the government's website for the updated TSA rules and regulations. I am sure you will find new things to add to this list and some things you will not use, but this gives you a start when looking around wondering what do I pack and where do I begin.

Enjoy your cruise vacation!

OVERVIEW

This is a checklist that you can use to follow along as you make your cruise vacation plans. It is basically a "quick view" of the book in a condensed version. Use this to keep organized as you plan your cruise and enjoy your cruise vacation.

- Cruise Vacation:
    - Length of cruise vacation (3 day, 4, 5, 6, 7, 8, 9, 10, 11, 12, 13, 14, etc)
    - Cruise Destination:
        - Caribbean
        - Europe
        - Alaska
        - South America
        - Mexican Riviera
        - Hawaii
        - Asia
        - Australia
        - Bermuda
        - South Pacific
        - East Coast Fall Foliage
        - Other

Beginner's Guide to Cruising

- Ship size/passenger capacity:
  - Mega-liner – 4,000+ passengers
  - Large – 1,000 – 4,000 passengers
  - Medium – 500 – 1,000 passengers
  - Small – 50 – 500 passengers
- Style:
  - Adventurous
  - Laid back and relaxed
  - Theme cruise
  - Eco – cruise
  - Historical
  - Sport
  - Naturalist/Exploration
  - Formal
  - Informal
  - Family
  - Children
  - Romantic
  - Culinary
  - Entertainment
- Accommodations:
  - Interior Cabin
    - No window – the traditional definition of an interior cabin
    - With a window – new option made available in 1999
    - With a balcony – new trend starting in 2009

- o Outside Cabin
  - o Large window
  - o Small window
  - o Balcony
  - o Suite
- Purchasing:
  - o Book your own airfare, or
  - o Let the cruise line book your airfare
  - o Drive to the port instead of flying
  - o Purchase your own travel insurance, or
  - o Purchase the cruise line's travel insurance
  - o Request a copy of your insurance policy
  - o Book your own hotel room if you are arriving early or leaving later, or
  - o Let the cruise line book your hotel accommodations
  - o Purchase transfer tickets from the airport to the ship – roundtrip, or
  - o Find your own transportation to and from the ship
- Finalize:
  - o Make your initial deposit
  - o Choose a cabin number, or
  - o Let the cruise line choose your cabin number
  - o Choose your dining option (late seating or early seating)

- o Discuss any special dietary needs
- o Confirm the cruise line's booking number
- Now that you have booked:
  - o Pre-register on the cruise line's website
  - o Check that all information is correct (name spelling, addresses, etc)
  - o Confirm your booking number in the cruise line's reservation system
  - o Obtain a Passport
  - o Book your shore excursions
- When your cruise packet arrives (approx. 30-45 days prior to departure):
  - o Check that all information is accurate (spelling, reservation #, cabin #, air, etc)
  - o Fill out any forms that are required
  - o Check that all information is included (air vouchers, transfers, shore tours, etc)
  - o Fill out provided luggage tags
  - o Print a TSA list of allowable items in your checked luggage and your carry-on
- Pack:
  - o Use the packing list provided in this book
  - o Check the cruise line's reference guide provided in your cruise packet
- Arriving:
  - o Check in with the cruise line rep at the airport

- o Have all needed medicines with you
- o Check in at the cruise terminal
- o Check your cabin
- o Check your daily newsletter for upcoming events and important information
- o Explore the ship
- o Attend the life boat drill
- o Enjoy the sail away party
- Your cruise vacation begins:
  - o Enjoy, relax, and have fun
- Last full day of vacation:
  - o Attend debarkation briefing
  - o Pack – again
  - o Leave out all needed medications and clothes for the next day
  - o Fill out new luggage tags
  - o Fill out the Customs Declaration form
  - o Fill out the comment card/survey
  - o Gratuities
  - o Review your itemized list of purchases you made on the ship
  - o Determine where you will gather the next morning for the debarkation process
- Last morning:
  - o Gather in your designated lounge
  - o Depart the ship – for the last time
  - o Find your luggage
  - o Off to the airport or hotel
  - o Have a safe journey home

CPSIA information can be obtained at www.ICGtesting.com
Printed in the USA
LVOW10s1920240314

378693LV00024B/836/P